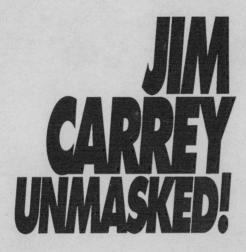

JIM
CARREY
UNMASKED!

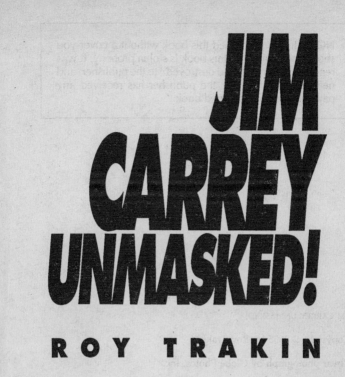

JIM CARREY UNMASKED!

ROY TRAKIN

ST. MARTIN'S PAPERBACKS

JIM CARREY UNMASKED!

Copyright © 1995 by Roy Trakin.

Cover photograph by Globe Photos, Inc.

All rights reserved. No part of this book may be used or reproduced in any manner whatsoever without written permission except in the case of brief quotations embodied in critical articles or reviews. For information address St. Martin's Press, 175 Fifth Avenue, New York, N.Y. 10010.

ISBN: 0-312-95728-9

Printed in the United States of America

St. Martin's Paperbacks edition / July 1995

10 9 8 7 6 5 4 3 2 1

This is dedicated to my wonderful wife, Jill Merrill, and my two children, Taylor Max and Tara Paige, whom I love more than anything in the world; my family: my mother and father, my sister Janet, my mothers- and fathers-in-law Jane and John, Lenny and Carol, my "brother" Eric and his family . . .

ACKNOWLEDGMENTS

SPECIAL THANKS TO: Joey Gaynard, Phil Roy, Scott Steen, Louie Lista, Allison Stewart, Dominic Griffin, Madeleine Morel, Amy Kolenik, John Rounds, Marleah Leslie, Harvey Kubernik, and the MTV and Fox publicity departments.

CONTENTS

Contents

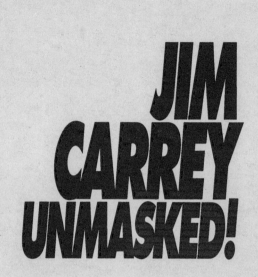

ONE

Fool's Gold: America Carreys on Laughing

"But when we play the fool, how wide
The theater expands! beside,
How long the audience sits before us!
How many prompters! What a chorus!"
                              —Landor, *Plays*

"Hain't we got all the fools in town on
our side? And hain't that a big enough
majority in any town?"
                    —Mark Twain, *Huckleberry Finn*

"Everybody loves a clown
So why don't you?"
                    —Gary Lewis & the Playboys

1

FOUR or five years ago, before Jim Carrey became the most popular comic actor on the planet, he would drive up to Mulholland Drive in the Hollywood Hills, overlooking the twinkling city below, and imagine that he'd gotten all the things he'd ever wanted. He'd sit there, arms spread out to the sky, acknowledging the cheers of the crowd, turning down co-starring roles with Jack Nicholson, being pursued by Martin Scorsese, ripping up multimillion-dollar contracts just because he felt like it. It was a time in his life when he wasn't sure he'd ever achieve the high goals he'd set for himself of stardom and worldwide popularity.

"What success means is being at the top of my

game," he explained to *Playboy*. "That's what I'm still looking for."

By refusing to compromise and following the stand-up comic's well-worn path to Vegas and beyond, he had cut himself off from the thing he did best—performing in front of a live audience. And while he'd ignored his stand-up career in favor of the promise of movies, none of the bit parts in films such as *Once Bitten*, *Peggy Sue Got Married*, *Dead Pool* and *Earth Girls Are Easy* seemed to be getting his career to the next step.

It was a recurring fantasy that Carrey repeated to several interviewers as well as to Barbara Walters on her nationally televised Oscar-night chat with him. Whenever he went on one of his jaunts, he'd carry in his pocket a check he wrote to himself for $10 million "for acting services rendered" and dated Thanksgiving 1995, telling Walters, as she choked back the sobs, that he placed it in his father's casket after his death.

The fascinating thing about Jim Carrey's overnight stardom is that it was at least 15 years in the making . . . and Jim knew all along he was going to get there. "I totally expected this to happen 15 years ago, so it is a little disappointing it didn't happen sooner," he joked with MTV's Chris Connelly on a half-hour special devoted to him. "No, seriously. I'm glad it took this long . . .

it would have destroyed me otherwise."

In fact, the Carrey tale is one of ups and downs, early promise in the form of the lead in a TV sitcom, *The Duck Factory*, when he was only 22 years old and several appearances on *The Tonight Show* and long stretches where he tried to shake the paralyzing demons which came from an unbelievable, almost Dickensian childhood. For several years, Carrey and his family actually lived in the back of a beat-up Volkswagen van while working as janitors at a Toronto-area tire factory. The performer's comic ferocity can be traced to the anger and humiliation he underwent in those years trying to find where he fit in.

Like one of his idols, Jimmy Stewart, in *It's a Wonderful Life*, Carrey would escape from his own frustrations in those trips along Mulholland Drive into a universe of his own imagination . . . precisely the world which he first allowed us to glimpse in his incredible, groundbreaking, rubber-faced stand-up act, then as "the white guy on *In Living Color*," and finally in a trio of historic film comedies, *Ace Ventura: Pet Detective*, *The Mask*, and *Dumb and Dumber*. And while his depression never prompted thoughts of suicide, there is a dark underside to Carrey's broad physical comedy that underlines the pathos beneath the clown mask, the despair behind the pratfall, the innocence masked as stultifying stupidity. "My focus is to forget the pain of life—to mock it and reduce it," he told *Newsweek*. "What makes Jim Carrey run is his desire to get away from his semi-lapsed Catholic past . . . a desire to outsmart the Grim Reaper at his own game by assuming a pleasing shape . . . whether that shape be Clint Eastwood drawling, "Make my day," or Sammy Davis, Jr., crooning "The Candyman," or Billie Holiday oozing "God Bless the Child." Jim Carrey's popularity can be traced directly to his "Zelig"-like ability to make his face conform to any shape as in his early impressionist days on the Toronto comedy club circuit right up to those Industrial Light & Magic contortions in *The Mask*. The audience is free to project their own fantasies upon the tabula rasa of his seemingly moldable quicksilver features.

To say 1994 was a very good year for Jim Carrey would be a heinous understatement. The guy's salary went from $350,000 to $10 million and the three movies he starred in, which came out in those 12 months topped $300 million in box office receipts. Like the putty-faced cartoon superhero he plays in *The Mask*, Carrey has seemingly come out of nowhere to become America's number 1 box office attraction. And while many point to his "triumph of the dumb" as a low mark in popular culture, we are going to show that Jim Carrey is a remarkable physical comedian, a throwback to the likes of Buster Keaton, Charlie Chaplin, and Harold Lloyd. (On *Regis & Kathie Lee*, Jerry Lewis compared him to slapstick comic Harry Langdon, the baby-faced melancholic American clown and '20s silent film star who was unable to make the transition to talkies.) Witness the opening kick-the-parcel sequence in *Ace Ventura*, the "Hey Pachuco" and "Cuban Pete" dance scenes in *The Mask*, or the karate scene in *Dumb and Dumber* for examples of Carrey's dexterity and grace. Not bad for a guy whose claims to fame include the fact he kissed a plunger and made his asshole talk.

It's a Friday night in Atlanta, February 4, 1994. Carrey's in Atlanta to do a stand-up gig at a local concert hall. He summoned his best friend, Wayne Flemming, a fellow stand-up comic 14 years his senior who knew Carrey from when he was a teenager performing on the local Toronto comedy circuit. The two drove around town counting the number of *Ace Ventura* posters that were plastered around the city and looking in awe at the marquees which featured Jim Carrey's name in large letters. The two lowered their sights to see lines of fans streaming into the streets. They couldn't believe their eyes. That night, Jim sat by the phone getting in the returns as if it were an election. Saturday night, he hit the stage to the roar of 3,000 screaming fans.

"My hair is standing on end," he told the *Charlotte Observer*. "The act I give them is even weirder than 'Ace.' It gets to the point where I'm being an absolute babbling idiot."

By the end of the three-day weekend, Carrey learned that *Ace Ventura*, made for $15 million, had earned $12 million in gross receipts, enough to land it on top of the box office leaders, more than both *Philadelphia* and *Schindler's List*, the next two movies, combined.

Jim Carrey was just beginning to feel his power, the charisma which would not only launch three hit movies, but an appearance as the Riddler in *Batman Forever*, a pair of hit sequels for which he'd earn almost $20 million dollars, and a cottage industry spawning three Saturday morning cartoon shows, a CD-ROM, and a burgeoning songwriting career as well as continuing interests in drawing, painting, and sculpture. Not to mention a stunning new girlfriend in his *Dumb and Dumber* co-star Lauren Holly. Yep, by June, 1995, Jim Carrey was definitely one of the three hottest stars in Hollywood, along with Tom Hanks and Kato Kaelin, of course.

But it wasn't always like that. In fact, life was pretty hard for Jim Carrey, though he always found a way to avoid the hurt in his self-created comic world.

TWO

Growing Up Absurd

JAMES Eugene Carrey was born on January 17, 1962, in Jackson's Point, Ontario, a rural area outside Toronto where rich folks had summer homes, but the Carrey family lived full-time. He was the youngest of four children—an older sister and two brothers—born to his father, Percy Joseph, a soft, gentle jazz/sax clarinetist who briefly fronted a big band orchestra in Toronto before meeting his future wife, Kathleen, and giving up show business in favor of the more secure position of accountant when he was 16 years old. Carrey often told the story about how "he sold his saxophone to pay the bills to get my sister out of the hospital when she was born," jokingly adding, "Is that a TV movie or what?"

Although the family was surrounded by those who were more well-to-do, Carrey's father instilled in all his children the strength to never give up on their dreams ... ironically, as he had done, and what his son Jim would fight never to do.

By the age of three, young Jim realized show business was in his blood. He always has insisted he inherited his sense of humor from his father, who was forever cutting up around the house and playing practical jokes on the other kids. Jim was always trying to top his father or make him laugh. "I wanted to be just like him," he told Barbara Walters.

"We were the wildest family, I swear to God," Jim told the *Los Angeles Times* in May 1994. Visitors to the Carrey home were just as likely to get butter smeared across their face or find themselves involved in a Sunday evening cherry cheesecake fight at the dinner table. On Christmas, the entire family would run outside with stockings on their heads, wielding axes and completely freaking out passers-by.

Jim himself retreated to his room, watching Dick Van Dyke on TV and dreaming of stardom. "I would lie in my bed at night, staring at the ceiling, and wonder, 'What is it about me that's going to be different, that's going to be special?,' " he told the *Detroit Free Press*. "I knew I had to clue into something." He was extremely shy at school. The kids there used to taunt him by calling him Jimmy-Gene the String Bean. He didn't like it. He retreated into a shell, without a friend in the world until the second or third grade, when he discovered a gift for making the other kids laugh. It was a real turning point for Carrey, who suddenly realized he could do something silly and make people want to talk to him.

In the second grade at Blessed Trinity School, he imitated the Three Stooges for the Christmas play, cracking up his principal, Sister Mary Joan, who would fall out of her chair, laughing, on hands and knees.

He became an expert class clown. One teacher punished him by making him stay 15 minutes after school to perform. Little did she realize she was playing right into young Jim's hands. He'd chew up a pack of candies, then act like he was sick and throw up every color of the rainbow to the delight of his schoolmates.

Around the house, he desperately tried to please his parents and brothers and sisters by making them laugh. He'd do everything from taking a dive onto the floor after sliding down the stairs to running in slow motion. "It came from wanting to be noticed," he told a reporter. "My father was really funny, and I guess it was a competitive thing with him. But a good competitive thing. It wasn't strange or anything."

At about the age of eight or nine, Carrey discovered he could make the planes and curves of his face shift and quiver. He spent hours in front of the mirror in his bedroom practicing his different faces and voices. "You couldn't send me to my room when I was bad because I had too much fun up there," he told a Japanese reporter. "To punish me, you had to send me out with the other kids."

"It would drive my mother crazy," he told the Knight-Ridder syndicate about his penchant for mugging in the mirror. "She used to scare me by saying I was going to see the devil if I kept looking in the mirror and making faces like that. Or that my face would stay like that. Which fascinated me and made me want to do it even more, of course."

Carrey also discovered an early talent for mimicry. His biography for *The Duck Factory* claims his first impression was a soprano John Wayne at the age of eight. Jimmy began putting on shows for his family, imitating neighbors and television stars and contorting his face into weird visages. He desperately wanted to please his parents, hoping someday to make their lives "happy and beautiful." One of the bits hit close to home as he'd unerringly mimic his mother's alcoholic parents. Carrey's later comedy routine featured several bits about his family, including how his grandparents inhaled their food and how his mother would complain about smelling smoke in hell.

It would be a theme he'd return to when he played the troubled, alcoholic son who has grown distant from his parents after failing to live up to their expectations in the 1991 Fox movie, *Doing Time On Maple Drive*.

The daughter of alcoholics, his mother Kathleen began to imagine herself suffering from all kinds of diseases, a hypochondriac prone to depression.

"The illnesses were her medals," recalled Carrey in the *L.A. Times* about the woman he called "Mommsie." "After awhile, you just became used to it. We'd be at the dinner table and my mom would go, 'I have cancer,' and we'd go, 'Great, pass the salt.' "

Another escape for Jim was poetry. He'd write nonsensical verse that he described as "just weird."

He found himself driven to make people

laugh, to earn their recognition and love.

Carrey never wanted to do anything else. Despite everything that happened to the Carreys, his father never stopped being funny. Jim himself would watch Dick Van Dyke on television and dream of someday doing the same thing.

"It's weird. I can't imagine what it's like not to know what you want to do. People come out of college not knowing. I can't imagine that. It must be a horrible feeling. I knew what I wanted from the time I was a little kid."

Of course, before Carrey discovered comedy, he humped household objects . . . seriously. When he was eleven, Carrey went around humping things around the house, including a small green rug in his parents' bedroom. One day, with the family downstairs, he went into their room and "just started going at it." All of a sudden he heard his father coming up the stairs. Freaking out, he crawled under the bed. When his father asked if he was OK, Jim got up, slowly, with his eyes half-closed, and pretended that he had fallen asleep. Without missing a beat, he took his underwear off his parents' bed and left the room naked. "After that, I had to break up with the green rug," he joked to *Details* magazine.

At around the same time, his mother made

him take tap-dancing lessons. "I spent a lot of time trying to hide my shoes from the other boys on the bus," he told a Japanese press conference for *The Mask*. "Humiliation started early for me." But when he discovered his ability to make people laugh, Carrey began flourishing at school, excelling at ice hockey with his gangly build, earning straight A's and his classmates' approval through his riotous shtick. His tooth was chipped in some classroom horseplay—he took out the cap for *Dumb and Dumber*—he wore his red hair in a Prince Valiant cut and had freckles.

Then, when Jim turned 13, the family experienced a major crisis. After some 35 years at the same job, after rising to controller of his company, Percy Carrey was fired at the age of 51. The repercussions had a profound effect on young Carrey's life.

"It made me realize," said Jim, "that life offers no assurances, so you might as well do what you're really passionate about."

With his mother's condition deteriorating and his father out of work, the family was thrown into turmoil. Percy was forced to become nurse and caretaker for Kathleen, and young Jim helped out the only way he knew how, by making them laugh.

"When she was really in pain, I used to come

into the bedroom in my underwear and do my praying mantis impression," says Jim, whose lanky frame made him appear to be all arms and legs.

It was at this point that Percy, Kathleen, Jim and his two brothers—everyone except his sister—were forced to take jobs as janitors and security guards at Titan Wheels, a factory in Scarborough, Ontario, that manufactures steel tire rims. As Jim told Walters, they spent their evenings "scraping pubic hair off the urinals." Jim went to school all day and worked all night, a schedule which had him sleeping in class and avoiding his classmates' curious inquiries.

He was angry and had dropped any friends he still had. He'd look at homeless street people and understand perfectly what they were going through.

The family was forced to move into the factory-owned housing, which horrified and angered young Jim, who would lie in bed at night and plot how he was going to kill his enemies in very specific ways. Seeing his father reduced to menial labor after being the controller of a company embittered him. Jim was forced to drop out of tenth grade at the age of 16 to help support the family, which pissed him off even more.

He would carry a baseball bat on his cleaning

cart just waiting for someone to look at him cross-eyed. Though Carrey would never actually attack anybody, he'd sometimes smash machines and furniture. The bosses would come in the next day and wonder who put the hole in the wall, while Carrey would joke, "Aw, that ol' buffing machine got away from me."

For kicks, he once took two pairs of work boots into the men's room and lined them up under a stall to make it look like there was some hanky-panky going on. The whole place ran in to take a peak. The Jamaicans claimed it was the Indians. The Indians insisted it was the Jamaicans. Carrey smirked in the corner hoping for a race war. He was that angry. Tension increased within the family, forced to live on top of each other all night in shabby factory housing and work alongside one another all day.

"We were turning into monsters," says Carrey, "so we just decided to quit. We had nothing to go to at the time, either."

The family moved out of the factory housing and into a battered Volkswagen camper, which they parked in and around various camping grounds in the Toronto area. At one point, they pitched a tent in the backyard of Jim's eldest sister, the only member of the family who actually had a roof over her head.

"It was definitely *Grapes of Wrath* for a while," Carrey told the *L.A. Times'* Calendar section, explaining how he learned to make the best out of even the worst situation. His bleak surroundings forced him to work so that he would never have to experience that kind of hardship again.

It was at this time that Carrey took destiny into his own hands. Realizing his father had traded in his passion for a security which proved illusory, he decided he would go for the stardom he had craved since he was a youngster fantasizing in his room. After all, he had nothing else to lose. He couldn't go anywhere but up.

When his father lost his job and couldn't get another, it made Jim realize there's no such thing as security, so he may as well do what he loves.

Which, for Carrey, meant performing stand-up comedy. Working with his father, Jim wrote up a comedy routine, which he planned to debut during amateur night at a Toronto comedy club called Yuk-Yuk's. His mother dressed him in a yellow polyester suit, insisting, "This is what all the nice young boy comics wear. I know because I saw it on *Donahue*." His father dutifully drove him to Yuk-Yuk's and stood in the back as Jim tentatively launched into his five-minute routine.

"First of all, the polyester suit didn't go over so well in the hip underground world," recalled

Jim. "And then the owner of the club, Mark Breslin, liked to heckle young comics from the back on the microphone. He'd do stuff like go, 'Totally boring.' Or play excerpts from *Jesus Christ Superstar*, where they're going, 'Crucify him! Crucify him!' And they did. I got booed off-stage before my five minutes were up and I was devastated. That evening was the most awful experience of my life."

He stayed away for two years, but when he came back, in 1979, at the age of 17, he was ready. "Things had changed. I messed up my hair. No polyester. It was fine. Comedy had changed my life."

When he returned to Yuk-Yuk's, Carrey decided to concentrate on his comic impressions of people like Sammy Davis, Jr. and the Amazing Kreskin. Jim and Percy would drive 100 miles in the Volkswagen every other night for a chance to be center-stage. Together, they honed the act until it was razor-sharp. Carrey didn't just impersonate his subject's voice, he miraculously twisted his face until he actually looked like the individual. Among his earliest impressions were James Dean and hilariously accurate takes on Henry Fonda and Katharine Hepburn in the 1981 movie, *On Golden Pond*, which he performed for a Toronto midday news show at around the time of the film's release.

"At first he would just mug and jump around," says Michael Becker, a pianist who occasionally worked with Carrey in Toronto and later Los Angeles. "Then he began writing stuff down, shaping an act that was basically who he is today."

And, lest we forget, all this was going on while Jim was still living in the same Volkswagen camper which was taking him and his dad to those comedy gigs.

Wayne Flemming remembers giving Jim a ride home one night and being instructed to pull up to a van and realizing that's where Carrey would be spending the night. It was at this point when Jim began the painful process of trying to break away from the mutual dependence he had with his father.

His father would accompany him to the club every night, which became embarrassing when Jim started hanging around with other guys his own age. At a certain point, he was forced to tell his dad it wasn't cool for him to be there all the time. It was then Jim began to realize his father's own thwarted ambitions were finding an outlet in his son's suddenly promising career. "It was his dream, too," he told the *L.A. Times*. "He should have been a comedian."

But their desperate circumstances made it all the more difficult for Jim to turn his back on his family. He began to mold a successful act around his killer impressions. One night, Rodney Dangerfield caught his show.

"He was really sensational, an unusual talent," recalls Rodney, who put Jim on to open for him in Canada before eventually taking him to Vegas. "He could make his face into anything."

Carrey could have stayed in Canada and made a real good living doing stand-up, but people were urging him to move to L.A. It was a difficult decision for Jim, but the main thing was knowing his father's own artistic ambitions had been thwarted by a misguided search for security. His son wasn't going to let the same thing happen to him.

With the urging of his then-manager, Jim Carrey pulled up stakes and, at the age of 19 in 1981, moved to Los Angeles to pursue his Hollywood dream of stardom. Little did he know it would take him almost 15 years to fulfill that destiny.

THREE

California Dreaming: Carrey Way Out West

JIM had begun saving whatever money he could in hopes of moving to Los Angeles to try his hand in the comedy major leagues and places like Mitzi Shore's famed Comedy Store or Jamie Masada's Laugh Factory, the clubs he had only heard about when comics passed through Toronto to play Yuk-Yuk's. From the time he was a child, he believed in the possibility of miracles. And he'd need one to emerge from the shambles of his deteriorating home life, torn between fulfilling his destiny and continuing to support his family.

He recalled a time when his family was so poor, they couldn't afford to buy him a bicycle, so he prayed for one. A week later, there was a brand-new Mustang bike in his living room he'd won in a raffle he hadn't even entered.

It was all part of the wish-fulfillment Carrey would practice years later when he climbed the Hollywood Hills in his car, dreaming he was one of those stars he saw twinkling below and above. But this time, it would take more than wishing, dreaming, and prayer. For the first time in his life, Jim Carrey had to make a big decision—he had to leave his parents behind and follow his muse to Tinseltown. It was not an easy decision.

"At some point I realized it wasn't up to me to make their lives beautiful," Jim told *The New York Times*. "That was leading me nowhere. I started to do it for myself. Weird things. Don't try to please the crowd, shock them. If it's not funny, call it performance art. That's when everything started happening for me."

Ironically, Jim had to let go of both his personal and professional expectations to make his big move, artistically, emotionally, and physically to another city, another country, another life. Promising his parents he would send money back to them, he headed for Hollywood, the archetypal hick from the sticks who climbs off at the bus station with stars in his eyes and hope in his heart.

Accompanied by his Canadian manager, Jim

arrived in Los Angeles with a few phone numbers of contacts he had made in Toronto, $1,000 from occasional gigs and an openness that boarded on naïveté.

"Every L.A. comic or celebrity that came through Toronto, I asked if I could give a call when I finally got to L.A.," Carrey reminisced for MTV's Chris Connelly. "And they'd go, sure, we'll paint the town red. Then I'd call and go, 'Remember me? We met in Canada. I just got into town.' And they'd say, 'Sorry, buddy. I just don't have room for you in my life.'"

In his loneliness, Carrey turned to one-night stands. While we know he had an enormous sex drive from his admission he humped the furniture in his parents' house when he was 11 years old, there is no indication of any serious relationship. He was probably too ashamed of his circumstances to bring any girl home, but he undoubtedly embarked on several sexual escapades when he could convince his dad to let him go to the club alone.

Anyway, by the time he reached Hollywood Babylon, he was more than ready to sow some wild oats. When a pair of hookers approached him outside the cheap Sunset Strip motel where he checked in, he admitted, "I thought it was Sadie Hawkins Day. It was a complete other world. I watched the hookers walk up and down. It was like I had walked into some bizarre, X-rated movie. It freaked me out."

It was a scene ironically repeated in Jim's first starring role in the 1985 movie *Once Bitten*. When a vampire played by Lauren Hutton picks up the virginal Carrey in a bar and takes him home, he innocently asks, "Are you a prostitute? Oh, good, because I only brought $5 with me."

If Carrey was naïve when it came to ladies of the night, he quickly found himself sharing their world. He was lonely, single and bored, thrust into the middle of a surrealistic Hollywood scene.

But Carrey quickly tired of the sleazy, neon-lit Sunset Boulevard motel rooms. He got the name of a songwriter named Phil Roy from his manager, who had heard he was renting out an extra bedroom in his house.

"Jim just showed up at my door with a suitcase," said Roy. "I'd never met the guy before. He knocked on my door and ever since that day we've been best friends. The guy's like my brother."

Roy was a Philadelphia-born musician who grew up listening to soul by the likes of local legends Gamble & Huff as well as Motown and Stax. He attended the Berklee School of Music in

Boston, then came to L.A. when he was 21. In one of those hard-to-believe Hollywood success stories, he and his buddies stopped their car in front of Tower Records on Sunset Boulevard, where they recognized Warner Bros. house producer Ted Templeman. After cajoling the legendary A&R executive to listen to their tape, they were rewarded with money to record a demo.

"It was a magical day," marvels Roy. "Then I proceeded to learn what the music business was like, know what I mean?"

Under the name Carrera, Roy and his pals—actually Christopher Max and his brother London, sons of soul great Gene McDaniels of "100 Pounds of Clay" and "Tower of Strength" fame—recorded a single album before they were dropped and signed as the first act to ex-Columbia Records President Bruce Lundvall's new Manhattan label, this time under the name World Citizens. Roy went on to become a songwriter, first hooking up in a failed production company with ex-Culture Club member Roy Hay, then as a tunesmith whose work has been recorded by the Neville Brothers, Ray Charles, Joe Cocker, Barrington Levy, Paul Young and Pops Staples on his recent Grammy Award-winning blues album.

That first night, Roy and Carrey hit it off like

they were long-lost friends, even writing their first song together. "It's called the 'Ha Ha Song,' " chortles Roy. "We called it that because we were both laughing so hard when we wrote it. I just turned the tape recorder on and we had a blast. I still have it on tape somewhere."

The two found themselves at similar points in their careers, struggling to find the big break which would lead to their discovery by the mass public. "He is a loyal, incredible friend," says Roy. "We've been through 14 years in this town and to remain friends like we have is amazing. We moved away from each other and then, when things weren't going that well for either of us, we became roommates again just to cut down on expenses. Our professional lives were on parallel paths for a long time. He's always done the comic thing and I've done the music thing."

Phil claims Jim had a great ear for music, one which would reach its fruition when the pair collaborated on a song called "Heaven Down Here," which was recorded by New Age jazzers Tuck & Patti for their 1995 album "Learning How to Fly." "He doesn't really play anything, but if you saw his act in the early days, he did a lot of singing, a lot of music. He did incredible impressions of Billie Holiday, Tom Jones,

Sammy Davis, Jr. He's a natural musician and he can really sing."

Carrey immediately scored club dates in Los Angeles and Las Vegas, quickly gaining a reputation as the rubber-faced comedian, or in his words, "the singing comic impressionist."

New Jersey comic Joey Gaynard was a regular and an MC at the Comedy Store when he first met Jim Carrey back in 1982.

"I remember him showcasing his material," says Gaynard. "His manager would have him on every night. I thought he was just really funny. He had a very slick act for someone who came in from nowhere. He went over real big with the crowds right away. I don't know if I ever saw him bomb. He used his body like a rubber band. It was simply amazing.

"I remember him doing Henry Fonda and Katharine Hepburn from *On Golden Pond*, which had just come out at the time. He'd put on that fishing hat and wire-rim glasses, turn around, and he would literally be Henry Fonda. First time I talked to him, I remember telling him, 'Man, that's a great Henry Fonda.' He'd also do a great Tim Curry from *The Rocky Horror Picture Show*. And a bit called 'Wounded Swan Lake,' where he'd put his arm behind his head like a swan with a broken wing. He was really funny, an amazing contortionist . . .

"He was a really nice guy. I never, ever saw him throw a bitch tantrum. And he was real humble around the other comics. We'd all go out to eat after the shows and stuff and he'd be funny, but he wasn't an overbearing, always-on asshole. He was always a really cool guy. It's kind of funny to imagine him so famous."

Louie Lista is a musician, actor, and spoken-word artist who managed the Comedy Store and worked the door during the early '80s. Like Gaynard, he was struck not only by Carrey's raw talent but by his continued thirst to learn more about his craft and fulfill his artistic potential.

"What impressed me more deeply than anything was, as young as Jim was, he had absorbed so much from the classic films. We shared a real interest in the classic horror films of the '30s, with Lon Chaney, Boris Karloff, and Bela Lugosi. He had a tremendous sense of that classy, sinister sort of stuff.

"We used to talk about those things a great deal. I once brought him a book that included a storybook version of John Huston's *The Maltese Falcon* with Humphrey Bogart and Mary Astor. It showed the actual frames of the film captioned with the dialogue. I lent that to him and he was fascinated by it. I felt he was a real kindred spirit in drawing on the classiness of that period of films most performers his age are blind to. I don't know if all that has translated to his film acting yet, but you could see that sinister aspect to some of the characters he's created on *In Living Color*."

Lista was also taken with Carrey's elastic ability to become the various characters he would impersonate.

"When he'd do impressions, he seemed to transform himself into the actual person he was doing. One that particularly rang the bell for me was a hypothetical evangelist/singer who was so grotesquely exaggerated, singing a hymn, 'The Lord Jesus heard me singing and ran away.' It was very, very funny and wildly grotesque, just over-hamming and gushing. And it wasn't based on any real person. It was just part of his stand-up routine, not even one of his better-known bits, but it knocked me out. He had just picked up something out of a number of sources and made this unforgettable, kind of grotesque caricature of that kind of overdone, overacted TV evangelist gospel singer. It was overwhelming and totally convincing.

"He had a very good personality balance. Jim had a real high energy level he kept up most of the time, but he wasn't obnoxious like some of the other comics could be."

And while the atmosphere at the Comedy Store was pretty wild back then, Gaynard says Carrey steered clear of drugs and booze.

"Every night was a party back then," Joey laughs. "The Comedy Store was in its heyday and everybody drank and ran around. There was always a big crowd; it wasn't the cemetery it is now. Personally, I was more a drinker than a druggie. I don't remember Jimmy ever doing either, though. I'm sure he's been drunk sometime in his life, but I don't recall him ever doing drugs or even talking about doing drugs. I think his comedy just came from a twisted brain. That outer space mind warp thing he does so well."

Gaynard also saw the classical elements of Jim's act. And even though Carrey has insisted he's never watched the silent film work of Keaton, Chaplin, or Lloyd, nor was he a student of comedy, there are echoes of those masters in his work.

"I've always thought my best bet was to sit off somewhere by myself and create things," he told the British *Time Out* magazine in August '94. "That way things will be . . . honest. I won't be trying to express someone else's feelings."

"I think those are all people Jimmy respects

and was influenced by, even if he didn't grow up watching them on Saturday morning TV, like I did," says Gaynard. "He does have a great appreciation for the movies and great comedians, though. That was apparent when I first saw his act. He does slapstick, but it's all his own. He uses his physical prowess. I truly believe, in 20 years, when they teach the course at UCLA, they'll say, 'When we talk about slapstick, here's a guy who reinvented the form,' and they'll show his films just like they do Buster Keaton and Jerry Lewis and stuff like that.

"I think Jim created his own world. He wanted to be successful for himself and his family. He never had a bad attitude, though. Plus, he's Canadian, which is a little different than growing up here. He was driven in a very positive manner. I never saw him put down another performer.

"The first few times I saw him, I felt kind of competitive towards him because I was an impressionist, too. I told him how much I loved his Henry Fonda and he told me how much he loved my Sinatra. And I thought to myself, 'This guy's actually watched me!' I immediately thought he was cool. Even though I think he might have even done Sinatra in his act, too.

"The cutthroat world of the comics is in the

minds of the insecure and talentless. You don't
have to be a dick to get somewhere. You can be
a nice guy. You can be competitive without trying to cut the other guy's throat. If you can't
show your individuality with your work, you're
not going anywhere anyway."

Carrey was quickly climbing the stand-up
ranks, receiving standing ovations for his wacky
impressions, but it wasn't enough. His colleagues, guys like Arsenio Hall, Robin Williams,
and Sam Kinison, who shared a mutual admi-
ration society with Jim, were moving on to television, movies, and records. He began to find
stand-up comedy limiting, and his routines were
driving him "insane," he told *Entertainment
Weekly*." Carrey decided to reinvent himself and
start over from ground zero. Everybody told him
he was crazy, but he was determined. Jim didn't
want to imitate the famous; he wanted to be one
of them. And even though he was now earning
some good money, he didn't want to spend the
rest of his life entertaining drunks in Vegas.

People like the Comic Store's Mitzi Shore
warned him, "You're the king of impressions.
What are you doing? You're throwing it all
away!"

"I wanted to do something nobody wanted me
to do, which was ideas," he told the *L.A. Times*.

"If it doesn't make you happy, what the fuck good is it? I'll have a lot of money and feel like an idiot."

He began having bad dreams about strangling his mother, having children in danger in a room and being unable to get in to save them. One of his biggest nightmares revolved around doing his act in Las Vegas, with Wayne Newton himself in the front row. Carrey proceeds to do his Newton impression for the man himself, while everybody claps and points to the real Wayne, exclaiming, "He's got you down, man!"

It was not a pretty picture. Added to Jim's dissatisfaction with his career was the pressure he felt from the beginning to send money back to Canada to support his parents.

"My dad had kind of lost heart. He was kind of beaten down by everything that had happened so I really had to kind of tow the boat there. It wasn't a problem, but a couple of times it did kind of break me financially. I had to call them up and say, 'I don't know what you gotta do. Get on welfare or something, 'cause I have no more money.'"

When he began experiencing some success, though, earning upwards of $5,000 per appearance, Jim sent for Percy and Kathleen, actually inviting them to move down to Los Angeles to live with him. It was Kathleen's dream ever since she was a young girl to live in the States and Carrey was overjoyed to be able to fulfill that wish. Suddenly, her negativity disappeared and she began to appreciate life that much more. Jim's dad, on the other hand, remained "the happiest guy in the world," living out his own thwarted dreams through his successful son, as Carrey told *Interview* magazine.

But trying to be the perfect child in a dysfunctional family was all too much for Jim. He had to declare his independence personally as well as creatively. After a great deal of therapy, Jim finally realized his intense ambition to succeed came mostly from his desire to please his parents.

"I was trying too hard to be the good son," he admitted to Barbara Walters. "I wanted to be like Elvis. . . . I bought you Graceland, Mom. I finally realized I was mad at somebody I hadn't forgiven for something. I started realizing I was angry at them. At that point, I sat down with my parents and said, 'I'll help you out, but I gotta be on my own.' "

It was the beginning of a tormented period for Jim Carrey. Always fascinated with self-help and metaphysics, he threw himself into the Hollywood fascination with therapies, spiritualism, gurus, and other homespun religions.

"I don't think anybody should go through life without a team of psychologists," he's told more than one reporter. "I have been through times when I'm literally squatting in the living room, having one of those open-throat cries, where you're crying all the way to your butthole. I always believed I would come out of it, though.

"I don't think anybody is interesting until they've had the shit kicked out of them. The pain is there for a reason. A lot of times when I was in those depressions, I also had the thing going through my head that this is what I've asked for. I've prayed to God that I would have depth as an artist and have things to say. I've said, 'No matter what, keep me sane but give me what I need.'"

He began frequenting psychics, a phase which ended when one told him there was an evil curse on his family. He even dabbled in the benefits of colonic therapy. "It's OK," he said with a laugh. "But it's very strange, having this woman sitting there watch your doodad come out." He ran around town buying pieces of ribbon to fill the colors of his aura, then did Prozac, "which was very helpful ... You may worry that it doesn't let you feel the highs and lows that inspire creativity, but when the lows are so low you become immobile—you're not creating anything anyway."

Carrey also began painting and sculpting as well as reading New Age–styled books, a fascination that continues to this day, having digested such tomes as *The Road Less Traveled*, *The Celestine Prophecy*, and the works of C.S. Lewis. All that studying turned him introspective. He saw his future as a Vegas-style comic and it frightened him. The fear of winding up a slick nightclub performer began to paralyze him and throw him into a depression. With the encouragement of his manager, he decided to leave the world of comedy behind, take acting lessons and plumb his own life for material rather than rely on mimicking others. It would be two years before he returned to the comedy circuit and at that point, he introduced a whole new act.

In Carrey's new act, he worked completely without a safety net. As he told the *L.A. Times*, "It was like learning how to do a slap-shot in ice hockey with some weight on your stick so that when you do it without—when you finally get up there with some prepared material—you're that much looser. You're not afraid."

In 1982, though, when he'd turned his back on

comedy, it looked like he might not have to return, because the then-20-year-old got his first big break in another medium—as the star of a brand-new television series called *The Duck Factory*.

FOUR

The Clown Prince of All Media: Carrey Tackles TV and the Movies

FROM the beginning, Carrey told *Playboy*, he felt television was "insulting" and "horrifying." He didn't want to be part of anybody's sitcom. He'd go to auditions for shows and tell them how much he hated television, not exactly a way into a casting director's heart.

So it was no surprise that Carrey and network television didn't necessarily hit it off right away. There was the time he auditioned at the NBC studios in Burbank to join the cast of *Saturday Night Live* and caught sight of a guy in a blue blazer trying to work up the nerve to throw himself off a building on the lot.

"I got out of my car, started walking through the parking lot and I heard, 'Don't jump! Don't

jump!' The whole time I was in there audition-
ing, I was thinking, 'Is he dead yet? Is he dead
yet?' " he told reporter Frank Bruni.

In 1982, Jim had reason to believe his big break
had finally arrived when he was cast in the lead
role of Skip Tarkenton, the young and talented
novice animator in *The Duck Factory*, a TV series
slated for NBC about a failing animation studio
which got its name from producing the always-
on-the-verge-of-being canceled *Dippy Duck* network TV show. The program seemed to be
tailor-made for Carrey. The production company
was Mary Tyler Moore's MTM Enterprises and
the executive producer was Allan Burns, the
man who created the same *Dick Van Dyke Show*
which was such an influence on Jim growing up
as a young boy in Canada. The show was based
around the model of the workplace which
proved to be so successful for *The Mary Tyler
Moore Show* and Carrey's role—as the innocent
fresh off the bus from a midwestern town to become chief animator for the *Dippy Duck* show
only to end up producer of the program when
the company's owner dies before his arrival—
appeared a perfect fit, allowing him to play light
comedy à la Dick Van Dyke. In addition, there
were such veteran comedians on hand like Jack
Gilford, playing the alcoholic but still brilliant

director Brooks Carmichael, Jr., who was Skip's boyhood hero. Among the rest of the cast was Jay Tarses as the company's gag writer Marty Fenneman, who had done everything remotely connected to comedy writing, including soft-core porn and 250 funny cocktail napkins. Producer/ writer Tarses, with his partner Tom Patchett, went on to create such TV series as the Emmy Award–winning *Carol Burnett Show, The Bob Newhart Show, We've Got Each Other, Open All Night* and *Buffalo Bill,* with Dabney Coleman, then, on his own, did the critically acclaimed *The Days and Nights of Molly Dodd,* with Blair Brown. Tarses and Patchett actually got their start in comedy writing by meeting Carl Reiner, who played Alan Brady in the original *Dick Van Dyke Show,* on a talk show. Other cast members included Teresa Ganzel as Sheree Winkler, the bimboesque, Las Vegas–reared manicurist's daughter and deceased boss' widow, who had been married to company owner Buddy Winkler just three weeks before he died, only to take over as owner and self-hired receptionist for the ailing animation studio; Nancy Lane's assistant film editor Andrea Lewin, who plays Jim Carrey's love interest; Julie Payne's Aggie Aylesworth, the cheap studio production manager who vows to take over the studio; Clarence Gilyard, Jr.'s

Roland Culp, "the only black storyboard man in the business with a degree in dentistry"; and Don Messick's Wally Wooster, the legendary voice-over man with a repertoire of over 600 voices, though he's not sure which of them is his own.

The Duck Factory's gimmick was to weave animation in with the comedy, which jacked up the cost of making the series to its $17,000-per-minute price tag. Almost two years since Carrey first got the role, *The Duck Factory* was added to NBC's lineup as a spring replacement in April 1984 in the much-coveted Thursday night slot at 9:30 P.M., right between huge hits *Cheers* and *Hill Street Blues*, touted as the network's seasonal breakout hope. And young Jim Carrey, looking pretty much like the 21-year-old hayseed he was in real life, found himself right in the middle of the action. Unfortunately, the experience confirmed his fears about finding himself in the middle of the mainstream show business machinery.

Carrey complained the show never used him or his way of getting laughs like they could have. In fact, the show's 13 episodes were written before he was even cast.

And, of course, those were the only 13 episodes actually taped before the show was unceremoniously pulled off the air in July 1984. Still, Carrey exhibited enough charm and discipline to earn plaudits for his performance as the beleaguered straight man.

Variety's TV critic Richard Hack said: "To put it simply, Jim Carrey will be a star. His toplining of *The Duck Factory* . . . makes watching the program a genuine treat. There's a certain likability that Carrey adds to his scenes that could make even a funeral seem funny . . . Before the half-hour gets through, Tarkenton has a job and *The Duck Factory* has a star. . . ."

As for the show, Hack predicted the show's sophisticated whimsy and lack of belly laughs "may leave viewers wondering just what kind of comedy this is supposed to be," although it did prefigure such shows as *Seinfeld, Friends* and *Ellen* in its witty repartee. And while the critic praised it as a quality alternative, he also predicted the show's producers would have "the task of maintaining that quality, which is quite rare on prime time nowadays. The fear, unfortunately, is that it is a little like trying to save the condors. One mistake and you doom yourself to extinction. If applause helps, they've got ours."

It didn't and *The Duck Factory* was gone after 13 episodes. Maybe with Carrey's current stardom, it'll be revived on syndication, but don't hold your breath. Still, his mere presence in the high-profile TV pilot sent Jim Carrey's career into overdrive, as well as his personal life. In 1983, he briefly moved in with then 37-year-old singer Linda Ronstadt, the one-time amour of former California governor Jerry Brown.

He joked to *People* magazine that he broke up with her because "she was too young for me."

"I knew he was going to do real well when I saw him in *Duck Factory*," says his old Comedy Store pal Joey Gaynard. "I saw him do a few things in movies and he always came across well."

Carrey managed to nab his first movie role, a bit part in director Richard Lester's farce, *Finders Keepers*, which also starred Michael O'Keefe (currently Bonnie Raitt's husband and a star on TV's *Roseanne*), Beverly D'Angelo, and Louis Gossett, Jr. The slapstick comedy revolved around stolen money, con artists in disguise, bungling hit men, and veteran actor David Wayne in a hilarious part as the world's oldest train conductor. Lester was probably best known for his movies with the Beatles, *A Hard Day's Night* and *Help!*, but this effort was not one of the most distinguished in his career. It pretty much disappeared without a trace in a midst of critical indifference.

By the time of his next screen appearance, Jim Carrey had moved from the list of supporting players to the top of the cast in *Once Bitten*, a 1985 modern-day vampire spoof which takes off from the premise of the 1979 George Hamilton hit, *Love At First Bite*, except it moves the action from New York chic to Hollywood decadence.

Directed by Howard Storm, *Once Bitten* stars Lauren Hutton as an aging vampiress who only emerges from her gleaming white coffin in her glamorous art deco Hollywood Hills mansion with the help of her butler, played by *Blazing Saddles* star Cleavon Little in a hilariously campy, over-the-top performance, when she needs to suck the blood of a virgin. Enter Jim Carrey as Mark Kendall, a fresh-faced high school senior and part-time ice cream truck driver, who's about to pop with frustration over his inability to go all the way with his sweetheart, played by model Karen Kopins. The film is pretty much on the level of *Porky's* meets *Buffy the Vampire Slayer*, with a subplot from hell about two of Carrey's buddies who work at a fast-food burger joint by day and are trying like hell to get laid at night.

Critic Leonard Maltin called the movie a "bomb, an inept comedy, anemic." Sure, it's all those things, but the movie does offer a fascinating insight into the then-22-year-old Carrey's incipient talents. First of all, like *The Duck Factory*, the movie played off Carrey's incredibly youthful demeanor and virginal purity, something he still portrayed in his trio of 1994 box office smashes. There's a melancholic sadness in the early scenes depicting Carrey's sexual frustration that rings true considering his psychic turmoil at the time. There's also a touching awkwardness to his scenes with Hutton, where she tries to seduce him only to leave Jim with his pants around his ankles and a sheepish expression on his face. It is precisely that kind of nonthreatening charm which has made Carrey a box office star in these post-AIDS, sex-is-death era. It is a presexual charm, a romantic belief in uncorrupted love against the evil of sex.

And while the movie's script is filled with groaning one-liners and a generally unfunny script, the Jim Carrey subtext offers the careful reader some semiological treats. There's the famous Jim Carrey mug with a dress in a department store scene which echoes his slow motion run in a tutu from *Ace Ventura: Pet Detective*. There's his girlfriend's reference to him beginning to look like Jerry Lewis as he slicks back his hair and starts to wear black upon turning into a vampire, leading to his retort, "I thought I looked like DeNiro," twisting his face into the actor's with startling accuracy, a throw-away in a movie filled with them, but telling nonetheless. Then there's the climactic scene at the high school's Halloween dance, a remarkable pas de trois in which Hutton and Koppins battle for Jim's affections, as Carrey shows the rubber-limbed "Fred Astaire on acid" moves he'd later showcase in *The Mask*. Whether he's aping Michael Jackson's *Thriller* or playing air-guitar on his raised leg, Carrey is a physical dervish, a human pretzel who can seemingly bend his body at will.

Carrey's dexterity did not come easy, either. He was often tormented with back pain and aches all over his body. One day, he jumped out of bed and found himself unable to stand. "My legs felt like Ray Bolger's," he recalls with a laugh. "It was like I was off to see the Wizard or something. After a few days, I went to a chiropractor and he gave me these exercises I did faithfully every day. When I went back to him again, he said, 'I can't believe how you've healed!' And I told him I did the exercises every day. He was shocked. 'Really,' he said. 'Nobody really does that!' But I did."

His current assistant, Linda Fields, insists he still gets cuts and bruises all over his body from his strenuous style of physical comedy.

"He's black and blue, he doesn't know where he gets them. He's got a lower back thing and throws his back out on occasion. When that happens, he can be bedridden for days. There are all these consequences he doesn't even think about."

After *Once Bitten*, he returned to the comedy club circuit, determined to be not only a star, but an original. For inspiration, one day he went to see his idol Jimmy Stewart read from the Bible at the Hollywood Presbyterian Church, where he sat in the front pew with his jaw dropping like the wolfman he metamorphoses into in *The Mask*. After the reading, he lined up to meet his hero, hoping the star would anoint him as his logical successor in a quasi-John the Baptist baptism.

He pumped the screen legend's hand and, his voice rising like Stanley Ipkiss turning into his alter ego, "Jimmy, you are my greatest inspiration!" The object of his devotion blushed, then turned away without saying a word.

Carrey's Jimmy Stewart impression was one of the highlights of his set. He would always remark how the actor had a way of always looking on the positive side of things, then would launch into a letter-perfect Stewart at the apocalypse.

"Well, I guess we're gonna have ourselves a nuclear holocaust," he drawled, his face turning into the actor's aw-shucks grin. "Come over to the window, everybody. Look at that mushroom cloud. Isn't it beautiful?" All in the same tone in which Jimmy Stewart celebrated the merriest Christmas of all in *It's a Wonderful Life*.

When Carrey started doing stand-up again, he left most of the impressions behind. He adopted a stream-of-consciousness, anything-goes approach. He did anything that popped into his fertile imagination—ten minutes as a cockroach, a seeming eternity uttering a nonsense syllable, lying down onstage out of the audience's sight doing "snake boy."

"It was my expression, it was me," he said of the new act. He vowed never to repeat the same bit twice.

Some nights, he was on and other nights he'd face a mute audience. On one occasion, he appeared on-stage with nothing on but a sock over his Jimmy. "And if it hadn't been so cold, I might even have taken that off," he told *Details*.

At around this time, his old pal Rodney Dangerfield offered him a chance to be his opening act in Vegas. He came onstage with spiked hair and big red pants and just go off. Many nights, he got no reaction at all.

Rodney would watch him from the wings in his housecoat. "I'd come offstage and he'd take a drag from his cigarette, shake his head and say, 'They were lookin' at you like you was from another fuckin' planet, kid,'" said Carrey, with an impeccable Dangerfield impression.

It was during this time that Carrey met 26-year-old Melissa Womer, an aspiring actress from Altoona, Pennsylvania, who was waitressing at the Comedy Store. Melissa told *People* magazine: "As soon as I saw him, he seemed like family."

The other comics had noticed the pretty Womer, but it was Jim who moved in first.

"She was a really good-looking girl," recalled Joey Gaynard. "I knew her a little bit. She used to work out at a gym where a couple of my wrestling friends used to work out. She knew one of the guys there and we started talking. All I know is she was cute, and the next thing I know Jimmy was with her. And I thought, that makes sense. After all, I look like John Belushi and he's kind of a handsome, tall guy."

The two were married in March 1986 and a year later had a baby girl named Jane. "Some show people are always on," she told a reporter. "Jim isn't. He's serious and quiet, always thinking and creating."

Meanwhile, Jim's career continued on the up-swing. He landed a role in Francis Ford Coppola's highly touted *Peggy Sue Got Married*, starring Kathleen Turner as a woman who attends her twenty-fifth high school reunion and ends up going back in time, where she first met her now-divorced husband, Nicolas Cage. The film shared the plot twist of the previous year's smash, *Back to the Future*, as Turner tampered with the past in an ill-fated attempt to change history. The critics were fairly kind—Leonard Maltin praised Turner's "radiant star power," but said the movie left "far too many plot threads dangling" and termed Cage's mannered performance "annoying" and "a debit."

Coming on the heels of *Back To the Future*, with a troubled production history that included another leading lady (Debra Winger) and two other directors before Coppola came aboard, the movie turned out to be a bit of a box office disappointment. Still, it was the most prestigious part that young Jim Carrey had garnered to date. Jim played Walter Getz, the Cage character's best pal in the movie, a role that carried over into real life as Carrey and Cage launched a friendship that would continue into the present.

A crew-cut, wire-rim-glasses–wearing Carrey appears in the film's first scene at the high school reunion as the dentist he ended up becoming, sharing a line of coke and remarking how lucky he is to be able to get his hands on the pharmaceutical brand. "I could drill my own teeth with this stuff," he jokes. There are other bits of Carreyana in the scene where Turner wakes up 25 years in the past, having just given blood for a school drive. Jim wraps his arm around his head in the gesture he used to do his "Wounded Swan Lake" bit and quips, "I'm a little worried about the side effects."

Later on, he gets to don a silver lamé jacket and join Cage for a doo-wop rendition of Dion & the Belmonts' "I Wonder Why," in which he exhibits traces of his rubber-limbed mugging. He also gets to do a fake gag routine that is vintage Jim.

FIVE

The Calm Before the Storm: Carrey Breaks Through

"A lot of people don't remember that Jim didn't work for three or four years," recalls his good friend Phil Roy. "People don't know what a struggle it was for Jim. His management kept telling him he was a movie star and shouldn't do stand-up anymore. It was kind of the thing I was going through, moving from a performer to a songwriter."

Jim grew increasingly frustrated with his inability to land the type of roles which would get him more attention. He devoted himself to his new wife and daughter, but his lack of success was getting to him. This was the time he'd take those drives up to Mulholland Drive and pretend he was the biggest star in Hollywood. It was also around this time he wrote out that infamous $10-million check to himself, dated Thanksgiving '95 and marked "for acting services rendered."

He continued to search for answers, once joining his pals Nicolas Cage and Crispin Glover to visit the Hollywood Boulevard Church of Scientology even though he never intended to join.

"He's like a human sponge," Cage told *Entertainment Weekly*. "He absorbs everything around him."

When the three entered the Church, it turned into a real scene, according to Carrey.

"These Scientology people thought they had died and gone to heaven," he recalled. "They led us into this little theater and showed us the Scientology promotional film and I watched Karen Black and different celebrities with glazed looks in their eyes talking about how Scientology saved their lives, saying things like, 'I'm not working, but I'm happy!' It was utterly frightening."

Of course, Carrey wasn't exactly unemployed, but his film work was sporadic and he refused to go back to the comedy circuit except for an occasional gig.

Two years passed after 1986's *Peggy Sue Got*

Married before Carrey met an unlikely benefactor in Clint Eastwood, someone he'd often done an impression of in his act. Perhaps Eastwood caught the homage at the Comedy Store or Laugh Factory one night. Or maybe he saw the bit on HBO's *Comedy Store* special, on which Jim was featured. At any rate, Eastwood and his long-time pal, director Buddy Van Horn, cast Carrey in the superstar's next two features, 1988's *The Dead Pool* and the following year's *Pink Cadillac*.

Carrey's role in *The Dead Pool*, the fifth and thus far final installment of Eastwood's famed *Dirty Harry* series was memorable. He played the junkie rock star Johnny Shakes, the first victim of what was to be revealed as a bizarre death threat list and betting "pool" being investigated by Eastwood's Harry Callahan of the San Francisco Police Department.

Jim went back to his skill as a musical impressionist to create the flamboyant Shakes, complete with stud bracelets, tight leather pants, a forked hair cut, and a crucifix hanging on his smooth bare chest. Carrey lip-syncs to Guns N' Roses' "Welcome to the Jungle," one of several ironies and/or coincidences. The use of "Jungle" represented a real breakthrough for Guns N'

Roses, a group which had toiled just down the block from Carrey on the same Sunset Strip rock circuit which included both the Comedy Store and the Laugh Factory. When we meet Shakes he is crooning alongside what looks like the Bride of Frankenstein laying in bed, but in this context, could well be Carrey's own hypochondriac mother pining away. Outside the window shines a neon sign, "Hotel Satan," the name of the film-within-a-film, but also a recurring symbol in Carrey's own life, from his comic bits about his mother smelling fire in hell and his father losing a lit cigarette down his shirt to his ultimate creation of Fire Marshal Bill, a product undoubtedly of his Catholic upbringing.

The rock video/film is being directed by Liam Neeson, who turns out to be the killer behind *The Dead Pool*, and his name is Peter Swan; ironically "Wounded Swan Lake," which incorporates his trademark gesture of wrapping his arm around his head so that it looks like his arms are at right angles to one another, is one of Carrey's most famous bits.

Carrey uses his relatively brief screen time to its maximum effect. He is completely convincing as Shakes, doing just that as he acts out the part of an addict needing a fix. He retires to his trailer to shoot up, which he proceeds to do with alarming realism, relaxing his body as he enjoys the high. When Neeson enters his trailer, Carrey goes from a familiar, laconic junkie greeting to terror when the killer shoves poison down his throat. Jim then gets to do the death rattle as the camera pans up to the poster for the movie, which has the tag line, "You check in. You die." He even get to lie there with his eyes open as Eastwood and his partner inspect him in the follow-up scene before there's a direct cut from his lifeless corpse to a meat market. As death scenes go, it's pretty memorable, and an exquisite example of what Jim could do given just a little room to have fun with a part.

"Less is more, less is more, all the time I would hear, less is more," Carrey told a British reporter about people telling him to cut down on his faces and physical comedy through his career. "It's funny that the things people are annoyed with the most are the things that get popular." When Jim worked with Clint Eastwood, the legendary actor admitted the old-line Hollywood producers would complain his voice was hopeless, and that the very thing people tell you to stop doing is what eventually you become known for. "Anybody who is in the teaching game is trying to . . . smooth things off, but the rough edges are what make you special."

And as much as Hollywood would have liked to polish Jim Carrey's wildness, the comic continued to follow his muse . . . back into the stand-up world. He realized the comedy stage was the only place where he could really control and harness the thousands of characters which ran through his fertile imagination. By the time he was cast in a small part as a stand-up comedian for a scene inside a Reno casino with Clint Eastwood and Bernadette Peters in *Pink Cadillac,* Carrey was pretty much resigned to returning to the Comedy Stores and Laugh Factorys of the world. In the movie, he does his Elvis impersonation, singing "Blue Suede Shoes," but with an unforgettable twist—pulling the short-sleeves of his T-shirt down to his wrists, he does the King as a thalidomide baby with flippers, waving his hands in time to the music, as Peters pulls Eastwood out of the club, sneering, "I've had enough of this Elvis tribute." It's no wonder Carrey gave up on the movies—they didn't know what to do with him.

Still, the grueling comedy circuit—with its series of one-night stands and travel—took its toll on the young husband and father, taking him away from his family for long stretches that increased his guilt-ridden conscience.

Carrey told *Dramalogue* he found the grind tiring, often finding himself "completely miserable" until he hit the stage. Once there, he was in his element, on his own. That part, and meeting new people, he loved. He likened performing to "getting high without the drugs."

He went on to describe his comic spewing as the equivalent of moving his bowels, complete with sound effects. Finding himself on the toilet before a show, he'd joke that "stand-up comedy keeps you regular." Making noise as if his stomach was grumbling, he compared performing to a colonic. "I find myself sitting there going, 'Why do I do this? What am I doing?' It's just a crazy way to make a living."

This from a man who tried to solve his psychological problems through enemas. Despite his lack of a breakthrough success, Carrey was addicted to entertainment and thoroughly convinced his arrival was just around the corner.

He described himself and everybody in show business as a gold miner searching for little nuggets, like an appearance on Johnny Carson. "Once you get your first nugget, man, you're hooked for life."

Carrey finally grabbed that nugget with his appearance in Julien Temple's 1989 campy sci-fi satire, *Earth Girls Are Easy*. Temple was a British

rock video director who had done MTV clips for
such artists as the Rolling Stones, the Kinks, and
Culture Club after his much-acclaimed graduate
thesis film about the Sex Pistols, 1980's *The Great
Rock and Roll Swindle*, called the "*Citizen Kane* of
rock movies" by Mykal Gilmore. Rewarded with
one of the largest budgets in British film history
for 1986's *Absolute Beginners*, his homage to the
'50s American musical starring David Bowie,
Ray Davies, and Sade Adu went belly-up in the
U.S.

Three years later, he was back with *Earth Girls
Are Easy*, an amiably cheesy spoof of '50s sci-fi
cartoon comedies like Jerry Lewis' *Visit to a Small
Planet* and studio directors like Frank Tashlin
and Norman Taurog, starring Geena Davis as a
frustrated Valley girl manicurist who gets swept
off her feet by three aliens who crash in her
swimming pool, including future-husband-to-be
Jeff Goldblum, Jim Carrey, and, most importantly, comic Damon Wayans, brother of Keenen
Ivory Wayans, the man who was about to create
In Living Color.

The film received plenty of pre-release publicity, thanks to a heavily hyped soundtrack album
and MTV satirist Julie Brown's presence as
scriptwriter and co-star. Carrey was cast as Wip-

loc, Alien #2, and actually billed second to Geena Davis, ahead of Goldblum. Today, the movie is largely known as the launching pad for Davis, whose ditsy but proud portrayal of Valerie struck a note for female self-sufficiency that unfortunately wasn't held up by Julie Brown as her man-crazed boss at the wonderfully named Curl Up & Dye beauty salon. That, and as the place where Davis and Goldblum first met. And where Jim Carrey got to know Wayans.

Having previously known Damon from the Hollywood comedy circuit, Carrey got to know him a whole lot better when the two played a pair of fuzzy-suited aliens who were always threatening to make complete fools of themselves in their unbelievably low-rent costumes. The absurdity of the assignment gave the two comics an indelible bond . . . and a chance to appreciate one another's work.

Saddled with a bright-red, furry body suit, stripes across his face, a ridiculous football pith helmet and a kitsch codpiece, not to mention having to speak for most of the movie in a distorted gibberish translated by subtitles, it's rather amazing that Jim Carrey makes any impression at all as Wiploc. But his subtle physical performance—all suggestion, gesture, and nuance, as well as the tried-and-true Jerry Lewis-isms—is one of the film's few delights. As an alien gradually discovering and mimicking his surroundings, the role is perfect for Carrey's idiot savant, blank slate persona, sorta *Being There* meets *Forrest Gump*.

Carrey and Wayans spent a great deal of time giving the nonsensical language some kind of internal consistency. Carrey joked with MTV's Chris Connelly: "It was hilarious. I took it so seriously. Damon would just crack up. I'd argue with him that it shouldn't be 'Yakatakatokay' but 'Trayhldockalocka.' "

There are several great Carrey mugs when Geena Davis shows him how to flush a toilet and when he and the fellow aliens explore her '50s suburban tract home. Later on, the aliens are seen watching Jerry Lewis in *The Nutty Professor* and then James Dean in *Rebel Without a Cause*, a scene Carrey takes whole from his stage act to use later in the movie, amazingly contorting his face into the actor's for the famous line, "You're tearing me apart!" As an alien who quickly learns to adapt through imitation, it is the perfect use of his uncanny skill.

Eventually, Carrey and company get makeovers (natch) into spiffy Valley dudes, with Jim given a very flattering, sun-bleached blond surf look that comes in handy for the film's climactic sequence on the SoCal beach. Jim and Damon end up trying to man a Woody (car, that is) down the Pacific Coast Highway, with Carrey hanging out the window and uttering (in subtitles): "I'm one macho son of a bitch." Carrey also has a funny bit with a bubblegum piss-take eyeballing none other than eternal Hollywood starlet Angelyne before slamming into her famed pink Porsche with his car. And he gets to surf on a hospital gurney. Produced by Vestron in hopes of a theatrical hit which would make a subsequent video release more lucrative, the movie got caught up in the firm's financial difficulties and its distribution was erratic, though, ironically, it did end up a modest hit on home video. Nevertheless, *Earth Girls Are Easy* spotlighted Jim Carrey's skills, but, more importantly, solidified his relationship with Damon Wayans, so that when brother Keenen was looking to cast his brand-new comedy variety show, Damon didn't hesitate to recommend Carrey, even though most everyone else who would be featured on the program was black.

"Damon came backstage after I did something really weird and said, 'Hey, man you are one of the angriest people that I have ever seen,' " recalls Carrey. "And I said to him, 'Yeah, I guess

I've got that going for me. That's how I deal with it.' "

He would soon have a place to channel all that anger . . . and entertain millions in doing so.

SIX

Carrey on Fire:
"The White Guy" on
In Living Color

THE invitation from Keenen Ivory Wayans to join the cast of the fledgling *In Living Color* show, which would debut Sunday evening, April 15, 1990, on the brand-new Fox Broadcasting Network, couldn't have come at a better time for Carrey. The 28-year-old was married with a two-year-old girl and while he had no problem paying the bills, his parents, now moved back to Canada, were still draining some of that income. He was getting cramped for space in his North Hollywood apartment and still frustrated by how slowly his career was going. In his mind, he was a star, as those frequent trips up to the Hollywood Hills with that $10 million check in his pocket kept reminding him.

Keenen Ivory Wayans was a director/screen-writer actor who co-wrote, co-produced and appeared in Robert Townsend's 1987 breakthrough *Hollywood Shuffle*, which detailed the difficulties blacks had getting good roles and opportunities in the film industry. Townsend financed the movie himself on credit cards, as he decided to take matters into his own hands. Wayans, who went on to collaborate with Townsend on an HBO series, *Partners in Crime*, and with Eddie Murphy on the production and writing of his live 1987 concert film, *Eddie Murphy Raw*.

Townsend's example had a large effect on Wayans, who responded by writing, directing, and starring in the 1988 blaxploitation parody, *I'm Gonna Git You Sucka*, which featured a Who's Who of African-American performers, including Bernie Casey, Antonio Fargas, Isaac Hayes, the late comic Robin Harris, soon-to-be *Saturday Night Live* star Chris Rock, *Mod Squad* and *Purple Rain* star Clarence Williams III, a cameo by Townsend and future *In Living Color* cast members, his brother Damon, sister Kim, and David Alan Grier. It proved to Wayans the only way to do things was by yourself with family and friends. It was a lesson that wasn't lost on Jim Carrey.

Meanwhile, Australian press baron Rupert

Murdoch had set his sights on building a fourth television network in the United States to challenge the hegemony of CBS, NBC, and ABC. He had tried to launch the network a few years earlier by introducing a late-night show with Joan Rivers, which flopped spectacularly, and now he was trying to construct a prime-time schedule night by night. The man famed for putting nude women on page three of one of his Fleet Street tabloids immediately targeted the youth demographic with his programming, which was broad, vulgar, and smarmy, filled with double entrendres like the show which was the network's first unabashed hit, *Married . . . With Children*, which formed a potent one-two-three punch on Sunday nights with *In Living Color* and the hit animated cartoon show, *The Simpsons*, designed to grab the hipsters away from *60 Minutes* and *Murder, She Wrote*.

In addition to the youth demo, Fox set its sights squarely on the urban market, read: African-Americans. When they went looking for a black variety show for Sunday nights at 8:30 to be sandwiched in between *The Simpsons* and *Married*, Keenen Ivory Wayans was right there with the idea for an African-American version of *Saturday Night Live*, an outrageous ensemble show that would parade its ethnicity and go after the white establishment like no comic since the heyday of Richard Pryor. Just as *In Living Color* was tailor-made for Fox and vice versa, so was Jim Carrey just waiting for the opportunity *In Living Color* was about to present to him.

Despite his bad experiences with television, Carrey was willing to give *In Living Color* a try. It turned out to be the best place for him because they gave him free reign to develop his crazed persona. The only negatives were the censors, who drove him crazy, and the speed of television, which allowed him just a single take much of the time. That spontaneity, though, improved his ability to think on his feet. Performing in front of a live audience, he brought a danger and an anything-goes quality to his work.

And while his stage act was filled with impressions, this was the first time he ever got a chance to create fictional personas out of whole cloth, like the two which immediately took off—disfigured pyromaniacal Fire Marshall Bill and the sexually indeterminate, bikini-clad steroid casualty bodybuilder Vera de Milo.

He told Bernard Weintraub he went into the show to "sink or swim," having never really played characters before. *In Living Color* offered him a chance to demonstrate everything he'd learned in the past ten years struggling to make it.

The show gave him the opportunity to play all different roles, from maniacal to straight. He enjoyed stretching out, finding the complexity beneath even normal characters, revealing what was going on underneath. "Even the nicest people in the world have pain," he told *Dramalogue*. "So there's always a chink in the armor."

When the show began, despite becoming known as the show's only white guy, Carrey was not the only white performer. Actress Kelly Coffield was also part of the cast of *In Living Color*, but Jim still took a lot of ribbing about being the Designated Caucasian on the show.

"People wanted to know why I wanted to be the token white guy," he said. "It just fueled my desire to stand out. Desperation drove me, made all these wild things come out.

"In the beginning, colleagues would ride me a little bit. But I'd do it right back. I'd tell them I was closely linked to the head of the white race, and I could close the show down if they didn't stop it. I'd go, 'Just one phone call, man. . . . ' "

Carrey resented the implied racism in the question, but he'd just as soon deflect the jibe with humor, as he did when MTV's Chris Connelly uncomfortably posed the question of being the "Caucasian" member of the *In Living Color* cast.

"When are we gonna get past the color of our skin, people?" he asks in mock anger, facing directly into the camera. "Let it go . . . I thought when I came to this country, it was a melting pot. I guess I was wrong!"

But Carrey made himself right at home on *In Living Color*. He was immediately drawn to Wayans' desire to explore all kinds of issues, many of them too controversial to be shown on TV in the past. It appealed to Carrey's anti-authoritarian bent. He found the freedom liberating.

The show sometimes lapsed into bad taste. Even Carrey found some of the sketches mean, but he worked with the program's writers to produce bits that had "some kind of tact," according to *Dramalogue*.

On *In Living Color*, Carrey found a playground for a wide variety of characters. He'd pull out impressions of people like Michael Bolton, Pee-Wee Herman, Captain Kirk, and Ricky Ricardo, but it was his original creations that captured people's fancy.

The disfigured Fire Marshall Bill, a safety inspector turned arsonist, was a triumph of Carrey's rubbery-face and manic, single-minded intensity as the well-meaning Bill would demonstrate what not to do with fire and explosives and, in the process, immolate everything around him.

Carrey claimed the character came out of his act, where he'd fly around the room telling the audience they were over the seating capacity and try to shut the venue down. There are also traces of his father, whose well-meaning attempts at caring for his family ended mostly in disaster. The fire motif is something that runs through his work, and is symbolic of the burning flames of hell Carrey has feared since his days in Catholic school. Does he feel guilt over his own chain-smoking?

The first time he did Fire Marshall Bill, he told a reporter that he went home feeling like he was going to hell himself. But the bottom line was the character was funny. "Was the original impulse to do that evil, or was it coming from a good place?" he asked himself, admitting, "if somebody else wrote it, I'd probably think it was disgusting."

Vera de Milo, in which Carrey wears a halter top and pigtails like some Eastern European gymnastics champ who had OD'd on steroids, came out of somebody he saw at Gold's Gym when he started thinking about doing *In Living Color*.

He told a reporter many of his characters began with a spark of somebody's personality that he would take "as far out as you can . . . That's what this show is all about. It's caricatures. Occasionally, I play something down, but most of the time it's about getting the laughs."

In Living Color, along with *Married . . . With Children* and *The Simpsons*, helped put the upstart Fox network on the map by causing controversy and garnering publicity, both favorable and negative.

Carrey was just hitting his stride as a performer. When the show was taped in front of a live audience, Jim was in his glory, demonstrating the improvisatory techniques he'd honed after a decade on the competitive comedy circuit. Humor was still the way he conquered the pain.

With *In Living Color*, he finally began to reach his potential. For Carrey, laughter was the most powerful, organic drug of all. The nationally televised show was making him a household figure, if not yet a nationally recognized name. Carrey was now represented by a new manager, Jimmy Miller, the brother of *Saturday Night Live* star Dennis Miller and a hot new agent, Nick Stevens.

Proving he could stretch out figuratively as well as literally, Carrey appeared in his own

1991 Showtime special, *Jim Carrey's Unnatural Act*, then was cast in a rare dramatic role in the 1992 Fox movie-of-the-week, *Doing Time On Maple Drive*.

For *Jim Carrey's Unnatural Act*, the comic returned to his old Toronto stomping grounds to tape an appearance at the Theatre Passe Muraille for the Showtime cable network. It was the first time he got complete control over a project, which he credited to his own Jim-Gene, Inc., production company, a play on the name he hated so much as a child.

The moment Carrey hits the stage in front of the partisan audience, he's in control the whole way. The effects from starring in a nationally televised show could be seen immediately.

"When he first played the Laugh Factory, before *In Living Color*, the announcer would say, 'Jim Carrey,' and the audience didn't react," the club's owner Jamie Masada told the *L.A. Times*. "He had to prove he was funny. Of course, now he merely has to step onstage and the people are applauding and screaming for two or three minutes. I've never seen a reaction like it."

And that is precisely the response Carrey gets when he takes the stage before a partisan hometown audience in *Unnatural Act*, after being ushered on by the JIM Dancers—basically three people in foam rubber letters spelling, "J-I-M," who stumble around and sing the star onstage.

Carrey, resplendent in a multicolored knit shirt that looks like a signal flag from a yacht, basks in the crowd's adulation, even tossing off one of his patented caterpillar crawls with his eyebrows before launching into a routine about Canada that immediately gets the crowd to his side, as he riffs on an old geezer who "had to build an igloo to protect himself from polar bears and flying hockey pucks."

With the crowd going crazy, he does his patented wild simulation of having sex, his body bending like a rubber band as he says, "I think those subliminal motivation tapes are starting to make a difference. Of course I listen to motivational tapes. Think I want to get stuck in this dead-end job? No sireee! Not me!"

The routine is filled with the personal observations Carrey now concentrated on, as he creates fictional characters that seem real, rather than the caricatures of his impression days. He does a hilarious bit about an unctiously ecstatic "Praise The Lord" gospel singer ("My singing made sweet Jesus run away"), someone so happy "people would be tunneling under the street to avoid [him]." He imitates Elvis having an orgasm, then compares sexual climax to a "temporary vacation," revealing it's the only time he's "really, really free," stroking the mike as if it's his penis.

Carrey delves into his troubled family life for some of his most corrosive material, imagining his parents have gone to hell, which spontaneously leads into portraying his mother as she complains she smells something burning down there, than a brilliant physical contortion to show it's actually his father, waking from an after-supper smoke to realize the cigarette has gone down his shirt. "Or maybe hell is just having to listen to our grandparents breathe through their nose as they eat a sandwich," he muses, snorting into the microphone as he revives one of the earliest childhood impressions of his mom's alcoholic parents. "It's not a meal . . . it's a struggle for life itself."

Then there's the old man reminiscing about when he was a sperm: "Back in the cervix, I was Semen First Class," he says, saluting. The only real impression he does is when he pays tribute to his idol Jimmy Stewart as the eternal optimist, able to see the positive side of even a nuclear holocaust. "And the amazing thing is how something so magnificent and colorful could melt your face off." Jim praises Stewart and adds, "You have to look death right in the face," then lapses into Stewart offering the Grim Reaper a bowl of soup. In a split second, he's a TV evangelist, then a sobbing Jesus on the Cross, warning his captors, "You guys are gonna get it. Wait until my Father hears about this. . . ."

What follows is an eerie meditation on the thin thread of sanity as Carrey speculates about that inner voice which either pushes you toward or away from violence and insanity. "Y'see madness is never that far away . . . It's as close as saying yes to the wrong impulse." He goes on to say, "If it weren't for that little voice, I'd be in the shark tank at Sea World," delightedly flapping his arms in a foreshadowing of the scene in *Ace Ventura* when he does just that. There are glimmers of the talking asshole in *Ace* when Jim turns his back to the front row and pretends flatulence and of the karate scene in *Dumb and Dumber*, with his martial arts routine.

There are imitations of Michael Bolton, an Iranian pop singer, and Casey Kasem before Carrey closes the show by doing a guy walking into a singles bar, bent over backwards until he's literally at a 90-degree angle with his groin thrust at the blushing girls in the front row of the audience, uttering the pickup line to end all pickup lines: "I could care less, but my crotch would like to buy you a beer."

It was a triumphant performance, made all the more poignant by the death of his mother Kathleen before the show was aired on November 17, 1991, carrying a dedication "to the memory of Kathleen Carrey a.k.a. 'Mommsie,' " as well as "special thanks" to Percy Joseph Carrey.

The death of his mother seemed to free Jim up to do some of his best work. *Jim Carrey's Unnatural Act* showed how he was not just an impressionist or even a slapstick performer, but that his act had taken on a new, quite revealing edge of reality and edgy spontaneity.

He combined his physical comedy with verbal wit in the special, dazzling the audience with his incredible dexterity. Once again, he turned to his family as a fertile source of material.

"About a year ago, I was up in Canada watching my father," he said at the time of the special. "He was telling a story of some kind and he just began to look like a cartoon to me. I realized how animated he was. It's bizarre, and I realized where what I do comes from. Just expressing yourself that way."

And while his success pleased his parents, Carrey admitted "sometimes I get the idea they're never satisfied."

With the special out of the way, Carrey was anxious to move on to working on new stuff.

Ever restless, he didn't want to repeat certain bits just because the audience wanted to see them again. He was anxious to do something completely different.

Carrey got his wish when he was cast in the Fox made-for-TV drama, *Doing Time On Maple Drive*, his first real chance at a sustained dramatic role as Timothy Carter, the oldest son in what seems to be a picture-perfect upper-middle class family that is actually falling apart underneath the stern control of disciplinarian father Phil Carter, played by *Doogie Howser, M.D.* dad James B. Sikking and *Steel Magnolias* star Bibi Besch as mother-in-denial Lisa Carter. Toss in a favorite son (William McNamara) who comes home from Yale with his bride-to-be (Lori Loughlin of *Full House*) only to reveal his hidden homosexuality and a daughter (Jayne Brook of *Kindergarten Cop*) who is afraid to have children with her antimaterialist art photographer husband (David Byron of *Soapdish*) for fear of incurring the wrath of their father, who thinks they don't have enough money and you have all the makings of a movie-of-the-week potboiler. Still, it represented a real change of pace for Carrey.

"It's my way of throwing the hounds off the trail," he told *TV Guide*. Ironically, the movie's director, *thirtysomething* star Ken Olin making his feature debut, had no idea who Carrey was, having never even seen him on *In Living Color*.

"He looked like he'd just gotten off the bus from Nebraska and I thought I'd discovered this extraordinary natural talent," Olin said. "I'd never imagined he was a comedic actor. He gave a very honest reading. It was so sad. I think he understands the part personally."

Carrey earned the role by playing it straight. He managed to explore a different part of himself. When Jim first auditioned for the part, Olin stopped him midway through and asked who he was, and was shocked to hear someone so serious was a comedian.

"But I am a lot of the time. I think comedians are the most serious people on earth. That's how you deal with it, you know? A lot of times you're putting out concepts that aren't very acceptable. That's the trick to comedy sometimes, to be able to take harsh subjects and make them acceptable and funny to everybody."

Olin told Carrey's agent he was delighted to have him in the movie and was glad he didn't know his work before he auditioned because he probably wouldn't have even let him read for the part. "It just shows that you don't know a person necessarily by what you see on TV until you see them face-to-face trying to deal with whatever you give them," said Jim.

The film's soap opera elements are redeemed by Olin's taut direction and the realism of the individual performances, particularly Carrey, who is cited as a "surprise" by the *L.A. Times*, which says "the comic actor who regularly transforms himself into such wild oddities as the pyromaniacal fire chief on *In Living Color* . . . proves his depth with a poignant portrayal of the adult alcoholic son."

Indeed, Carrey seems to have tapped his own discontented childhood for the brooding Tim Carter, particularly in the scene where he confronts his father over not allowing him to drink during the day at the family restaurant. Jim runs through the gamut of emotions, from shame to embarrassment to anger to resignation in a stunning display of his acting ability. For most of the movie, Carrey slinks into the background, sullen, hurt and wanting to belong. His other tour de force is a scene where he toasts his brother's wedding and reveals the pain he experienced when he learned he wouldn't be best man. This is Jim Carrey stretching artistically, not just physically, and touching at emotional truths that ring even truer when you know his own background. It's a sure sign that Carrey still has plenty of depth we haven't yet seen in any of his comedies.

The movie aired on Monday night, March 16, 1992, on Fox, garnering a 9.4 rating/15 share, the largest score to date for an original movie on Fox. It ended up with three Emmy nominations, including Outstanding Made-for-Television Movie; Outstanding Individual Achievement in the Writing of a Miniseries or Special for the writer of the teleplay, James Duff; and Outstanding Supporting Actress in a Miniseries or Special for Bibi Besch. The movie had an encore presentation on December 6, 1993.

Carrey's star continued to rise with his role on *In Living Color*. The show became a fixture on Sunday nights along with *The Simpsons* and *Married ... With Children*, forming Fox's strongest programming block.

By the show's third season in 1991–92, Carrey's portrayals of Fire Marshall Bill and Vera de Milo were two of the program's most popular elements along with buddy Damon Wayans' "Homie the Clown," and the "Two Snaps Up" gay film critics played by Wayans and David Alan Grier.

With a steady income from the show, Jim moved into a three-bedroom Hollywood home with Melissa and his then-four-year-old daughter Jane, every bit the devoted family man even as he began to get recognized on the streets more and more. And as much as it delighted him, the attention also ate away at his desire for privacy.

He did tell a reporter, if somebody wanted to do a Jim Carrey impersonation, he would love it. But he began to find it difficult to go out with his daughter, even just to trick or treat on Halloween.

"I just gotta find a mask to cover my face up, so people don't go, 'It's the dude from *In Living Color*! Here's an extra candy—Do something!!' "

That kind of fame would eventually destroy his marriage. The kind of recognition he was about to get from his first starring role, in a little movie called *Ace Ventura: Pet Detective,* which he commenced shooting during the summer of '93 while on break between the fourth and fifth seasons of *In Living Color*. That little movie was about to change Jim Carrey's life and send him hurtling into Hollywood's fast lane.

SEVEN

Carrey Holds the "Ace"

IN *Living Color* entered its fifth season on Fox in the fall of 1993 an entirely different show. Keenen Ivory Wayans had left the show in a dispute with Fox over ownership and direction of the show, and he took brothers Damon and Marlon and sister Kim along with him. The show was shifted to Thursday nights at 9:00, the same as *The Simpsons*, to battle NBC's *Cosby* ratings hegemony. Jim Carrey was suddenly the veteran cast member along with Tommy Davidson, Jamie Foxx, David Alan Grier, T'Keyah "Crystal" Keymah and Alexandra Wentworth as Anne-Marie Johnson, Jay Leggett, Carol Rosenthal and Marc Wilmore. From the "Only White Guy," Carrey turned into "The Guy" on *In Liv-*

ing Color, and began to be featured much more prominently on the show.

Fox kept the show's trademarked Fly Girls, but added a "brand-new" set and seemed to broaden the humor for a younger, teenage audience. And even though Carrey spent the summer making *Ace Ventura* down in Miami, he was firmly committed to the show.

As *Toronto Sun* reporter Jim Slotek told *Hard Copy*: "He doesn't forget his roots, his old pals, the ones who helped him along the way."

"He was always very cool when I ran into him," recalls his Comedy Store buddy Joey Gaynard. "He's not the type to go, 'Hey, I'm rich. Fuck you!!'

"A friend of mine who works at E! Entertainment producing segments for the news program ran into Jimmy at an awards show and Jimmy took the time out to give him an interview and everything . . . He was real nice, asked about the whole gang, including me.

"He's not ashamed of his past. He was actually proud that he came out of that whole thing. Like a lot of comedians and actors, the more creative ones come from these really shit backgrounds and you have to create your own work in your head to get away from it."

Ace Ventura: Pet Detective had been in development for more than five years. Jack Bernstein, the original screenwriter, dreamed up the idea while watching a "Stupid Pet Tricks" episode on *Late Night with David Letterman* with a dog that could go into a 7-Eleven, buy cigarettes and get change. "I thought to myself, 'What would the owner do if he lost his dog? What would he tell the police?'" he recalled for *GQ*.

His first choice for the role was Rick Moranis, but when he passed, several other actors were discussed for the lead, including Judd Nelson, Alan Rickman, *Wings* star Steven Webber, and even Whoopi Goldberg. The part was offered to Carrey for $350,000, but he only agreed to take it if he were allowed creative input into the character.

Carrey was shown the script after it had passed through several hands and he didn't like it much at all, but the idea of a pet detective held a certain charm.

"I wanted to see if I could take something like this, make it into something, shove it in people's faces and say, 'Yes, this is idiotic . . . and here it is,'" Carrey explained to MTV. "They wanted to change the name to just *Ace Ventura*, and I said, 'No, man, you can't apologize for a movie like this. You just have to go, 'Ace Ventura: Pet Detective. Be there!'"

Roy Trakin

Tom Shadyac, the film's 35-year-old director, was a former joke writer for Bob Hope who had basically been hired on the strength of a UCLA student film he made about "a guy's schwantz" called *Tom, Dick & Harry* before going on to direct *Frankenstein: The College Years* as a TV movie for Fox. He encouraged Jim to improvise on the set, to push the envelope of juvenile and ridiculous.

"We knew from the first day of shooting that we were way off planet Earth," says Shadyac. "We would either make or destroy careers. But Jim and I were in agreement that if we were going to light a stink bomb, let's make it a very unique stink bomb."

Morgan Creek CEO James Robinson saw the footage and knew enough to give them the freedom to explore the outer boundaries of silly.

"Look, if the appetizer tastes good and the first course tastes good and the rest of the dinner smells good, I'm not so stupid as to go into the kitchen and tell the cooks what to do," he explained.

"The scenes were written," Carrey told the *Dallas Morning News*. "But a lot of the stuff—especially the physical stuff—was created on the set."

Among those ideas: taking a bullet in the

teeth, using a plunger on his face, and making villain Sean Young a transsexual and revealing her penis to the strains of Boy George singing "The Crying Game."

The first sign that Carrey had a hit on his hands came at a test screening at a San Fernando Valley mall, as moviegoers yelled, celebrated in the aisles, and high-fived each other during the movie.

As he watched the dailies on *Ace*, Carrey was beside himself, but he still wasn't sure if it would go over or whether it would be too much for people.

When the film opened on Friday, February 4, though, no one could have predicted what would happen next.

"The date of its release was switched from February 18 because we didn't want it competing against *On Deadly Ground*," Carrey's manager, Jimmy Miller, told *US* magazine. "You look back on it and the timing seems like a stroke of genius . . . People were looking for funny movies as an escape from all of that natural disaster shit."

Just two weeks after the devastating Northridge earthquake, with storms ravaging the East Coast, and the theaters filled with depressing fare like *Philadelphia* and *Schindler's List*, *Ace Ven-*

tura, made for just $15 million, led the pack, earning $12 million in box offices grosses, more than the next two films combined.

"When the movie opened like that on what is traditionally a dead weekend, Warner Bros. went for the jugular by running commercials on *Letterman, Leno,* Fox, and MTV. Everybody got lucky and smart."

Disney CEO Michael Eisner sent Shadyac a congratulatory note saying "not since Tim Burton started his career with Pee-Wee Herman" had a director made such an impressive bow. Producers such as Steven Spielberg, Ron Howard, Richard Donner and Joel Silver all called on the director, who lined up his next project—a remake of Jerry Lewis's *The Nutty Professor,* with Eddie Murphy—at Howard's Imagine Films, to be distributed by Universal. All of a sudden, Shadyac was being offered $2 million to direct his next movie.

Ace Ventura: Pet Detective grabs the viewer from the opening scene, a parody of John Travolta's opening in *Saturday Night Fever,* with Carrey dressed as a parcel delivery man strolling along the street blithely kicking a package with something stuffed in his shirt. Knocking on the door of ex-boxer and snarling tough guy Tex Cobb, Jim delivers the package, which "sounds

broken," according to Tex. "Probably," answers
Carrey with a toothy grin on his face. "I'll bet it
was something nice, though." As Carrey walks
away, we soon realize he has swiped Cobb's tiny
shih tzu dog and replaced it with a stuffed animal underneath the shirt. That is how we meet
"Ace Ventura: Pet Detective."

There's something just a little off about Ace,
from his gaudy Hawaiian shirt, to his swooping
pompadour, sleeveless T-shirt, baggy pants
pulled up to his chest, and broken-down, smoke-
belching Monte Carlo. Ace Ventura's sheer joy
owes a little something to Martin Short's Ed
Grimley character, but otherwise is an original
creation, a combination Sherlock Holmes and St.
Francis of Assisi who eats pumpkin seeds like a
bird, barks like a dog, and whoops like a crane.

The plot revolves around the kidnapping of
the Miami Dolphins' mascot Snowflake from his
tank inside Joe Robbie Stadium the week of the
Super Bowl. Courtney Cox of TV's *Friends* plays
Melissa Robinson, a team executive, who hires
Ace to solve the mystery. Ventura is mercilessly
ridiculed by the local police force, especially
Sean Young's ball-busting Lieutenant Lois Ein-
horn, who growls at him when he tries to inte-
fere with the case, "Listen, pet dick . . . how
would you like me to make your life a living

hell?," only to have him grin and answer, "Sorry, Lois. I'm not ready for a relationship right now . . . but thanks for asking."

Carrey had a great time on the set with Young, teasing about her reputation as a bit of a kook.

"The first moment she arrived on the set, in front of the entire cast and crew, I said, 'Sean, we're not going to put up with any of your psycho crap!' and she just started laughing."

And then there's the infamous talking asshole bit, where he tries to pry some information out of the harried cop played by rapper Tone Loc. "Excuse me, I'd like to 'ass' you a few questions," he says, moving the cheeks of his butt as if they were speaking. "Afraid I'll make a stink? Do you have a mint. Perhaps some Binaca?" And then he starts crooning, opera-style, "Asshole-a mio." Guess you hadda be there. Anyway, the bit had its origins when Carrey was having an argument with *In Living Color* creator Keenen Ivory Wayans, so he simply bent over and conducted a read-through of the scene through his buttocks.

Carrey explained to reporter Michael Kaplan it was something he'd do if he were pissed off about something. "When you write something like that in a script, you get a lot of people wondering. Are you really going to do that? But that's what captures an audience: things that have never been done before. Until *Ace Ventura*, no one had considered talking through his ass."

The movie gets more outrageous as it goes along, with Carrey using every trick in a comic arsenal he had built up for the past 15 years preparing for this moment. One minute he's Scotty from *Star Trek*, the next he's Richard Nixon, Zelda Rubinstein, the tiny exorcist from *Poltergeist* or Boris Karloff. He reprises his old childhood bit of running in slow motion and backwards in a tutu as he masquerades as a psychotic football player trying to find clues to the mystery in a mental institution.

Soon Dolphin quarterback Dan Marino, as well as a slew of other Miami players, including coach Don Shula getting his hand caught in a mailbox by Ace, take part, with an absurd climax involving a transsexual ex-Dolphin kicker who missed the potential winning field goal in the Super Bowl returning as Sean Young's police lieutenant to exact his/her revenge on the team. Or as Carrey puts it after the film's frenzied climax: "You've been a wonderful audience. I'll be here all week. Drive safely and be sure to tip your waitress."

Of course, not all the pieces worked . . . and some ended up on the cutting room floor.

"There was a dream sequence where I had my face pecked off by pigeons as a tribute to Hitchcock," Carrey told the *Charlotte Observer*. "It just didn't fit. But we didn't take out anything just because it was too outrageous.

"Anything that's not supposed to be talked about, that's taboo, is funny if you're outrageous enough. If I'm going to have a homophobic reaction to being kissed by a man, it'll be the biggest homophobic reaction ever recorded."

Critics pretty much earmarked the film for their year-end list of the year's turkeys . . . and it was just February. Both Siskel and Ebert gave the film a sold thumbs-down.

"Siskel doesn't realize that millions of people are watching that show, going, 'Y'know, I'm not sure what Carrey is saying, but I've never seen anybody do that before. This movie must be fucking wild.' Now I'm afraid to get a good review from those guys. I told Warner Bros. they should use it in the ad: 'Two thumbs-down—worst movie ever made.' How can you get a better endorsement?"

But those who looked beyond the juvenile script saw an amazing physical comic and a slapstick genius. The people who flocked to the film were not those who listened to critics.

Carrey himself noted that making a movie was

The man with the rubber face. (© Steve Granitz/Retna Ltd.)

Lauren Hutton sinks her teeth into young Carrey in *Once Bitten*. (© 1985 The Samuel Goldwyn Company)

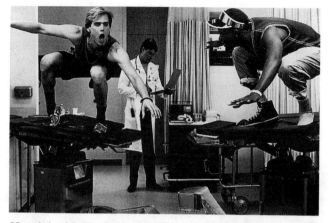

Hangin' with "In Living Color" co-star Damon Wayans in *Earth Girls Are Easy.* (Lorey Sebastian/copyright © 1989 Vestron Pictures)

Carrey in his early TV days on "Duck Factory."
(NBC/Globe Photos)

With "Friends" star Courtney Cox in *Ace Ventura: Pet Detective*. (SN/Globe Photos, Inc.)

Surrounded by his jungle friends in *Ace Ventura*.
(SN/Globe Photos, Inc.)

Beating up the mascot in *Ace Ventura*.
(SN/Globe Photos, Inc.)

With Milo, his canine companion in *The Mask*.
(Globe Photos, Inc.)

Carrey the heartthrob (above) spies the jaw-dropping beauty
(below) of Cameron Diaz. (Globe Photos, Inc.)

Tangoing with Cameron Diaz in *The Mask*.
(All Action/Retna Ltd.)

Sssssmokin'!!
(All Action/Retna Ltd.)

On the set of *The Mask*. (IPA/Stills/Retna Ltd.)

With Lauren Holly in *Dumb and Dumber*.
(Globe Photos, Inc./Rangefinder)

Alongside Jeff Daniels in *Dumb and Dumber*. (Stills/Retna)

Goofing off in *Dumb and Dumber*. (Stills/Retna)

Off-screen with new love interest Lauren Holly.
(Globe Photos, Inc./Rangefinder)

not about pleasing critics, but about doing what he thought was funny and trying to reach a mass audience. "Look, I'm not so unique that nobody shares my sense of humor. I know there have to be other crazy bastards out there."

Sure enough, the movie got great word-of-mouth with college kids adding such catch phrases as "Alrighty then" and "Reeeeealy" to their vocabulary, but it wasn't really the script that would've interested the French. It was Carrey's inspired juvenilia, the closest thing to Jerry Lewis we've had in years . . . at least since the heyday of Cheech & Chong.

"I used to be psychic about Jerry Lewis when I was a kid," said Carrey. "I used to be able to go, 'There's a Jerry Lewis movie on TV' and Click! It'd be on . . . I did that several times. When I first started doing impressions, I did a little Jerry."

Still, Jim's manager, Jimmy Miller, would rather compare his star to Robin Williams. "Jim also has this real improvisational element. Like Andy Kaufman, he has always had this high-wire act. He will go way, way out on a limb and work without a net."

Before *Ace* came out, Carrey's agent Nick Stevens—previously known as the guy who represented Jason Priestley—had negotiated a fee of

$450,000 from New Line for Jim to star in *The Mask*, a special-effects-laden movie based on the Dark Horse comic book series character. As *Ace Ventura* started taking off at the box office on its way to a more than $70 million box office gross, that price was beginning to look like a bargain.

Carrey passed on doing the remake of *The Nutty Professor*, which was being directed by *Ace*'s Tom Shadyac, preferring to bypass the increasingly frequent Jerry Lewis comparisons. He wanted to prove he could be Jimmy Stewart, a dramatic actor with comic undertones.

Director Shadyac agrees, adding, "He's a very accessible Everyman."

Even Carrey admitted to *GQ*: "Jimmy Stewart movies were my favorite. He could play a heavy dramatic role, but you felt for the character because he could smile at his own misfortune. As an actor, just being brooding all the time is tiring." He went on to complain about the then-current movie *Rush*, saying how he wanted "to slap those actors [Jason Patric and Jennifer Jason Leigh] . . . Even the most screwed-up person, even the most fucked-up heroin addict, looks up from their pit of hell and says something self-deprecating and humorous."

There was nothing humorous, though, about the breakup of Carrey's eight-year marriage to

JIM CARREY UNMASKED!

Melissa Womer, which occurred during the
shooting of *Ace* in Miami. Jim moved out of the
couple's Hollywood home into a high-rise apartment on Wilshire Boulevard in Westwood and
blamed himself for the split. Calling the bust-up
of his marriage "a cliché," he added that there
were reasons for the clichés. Once again, he compared it to the yin-yang which had ruled his life,
remarking how he was now "paying for the
good times."

It was a philosophy Carrey espoused to *Details*. "I used to be haunted by the fear of: If I do
this today, it'll have that effect tomorrow. You
can become completely paralyzed with fear,
thinking about karma and all that shit. I'm always worrying about [that]."

About his breakup, Carrey admitted that during *Ace*, his marriage was falling apart just as he
was doing what he'd always dreamed of. He
claimed it wasn't rewarding to live with him because he was like a caged animal, up all night
walking around the living room. "It's hard for
me to come down from what I do. It's like being
an astronaut. You're on the moon all day and
then at night you go home and you don't want
to take out the garbage. I can relax, but not at
the prescribed times necessarily, and when
you're married you've got to have time for this

111

and that and it's just . . . impossible."

He found it impossible to sit around the house and work on something when he'd just "touched the face of God." He admitted it was the kind of excitement he couldn't get "hanging out in his living room."

His newfound fame was also playing havoc with his role as father.

"I'd love to take my kid to Disneyland, but I can't. I tried it, and it was not good. I got the VIP treatment and everything, but it was, 'Hey, man! Do that face you do!' I try to stay away from that when I'm with my daughter, because I don't want her to be jealous of that attention."

He admitted that relationships would always be difficult for him, that he wasn't prepared to sacrifice what he had to in order to sustain one.

And why should he with his price going through the sky? A month before *Ace* opened, Morgan Creek was holding back on offering him a million for the film's sequel. Three days after *Ace* opened and grossed $12 million at the box office, he was offered a cool $7 million to star in *Dumb and Dumber* by New Line, who only a week before had balked at his $1 million asking price. Meanwhile, the ticket for the *Ace* sequel climbed to the $5 to $7 million range, more than Chevy Chase, Daniel Day-Lewis, Liam Neeson,

Anthony Hopkins, Patrick Swayze, and Gene Hackman command.

He compared the film business to the stock market, with him as the hot stock of the moment. Carrey insisted he didn't think about the money when he worked and that the business was like a "weird hobby" for him. "It's like looking at a Monopoly board and saying, 'Sure, I'll buy a hotel on Boardwalk!' "

Jim didn't want to be thought of as a money machine, insisting it was just a game for him. He wasn't apologizing for his skyrocketing salary either, because, as he put it to the *L.A. Times*, "I put butts in the seat and I make people laugh." He also didn't want the money to destroy his edge, pointing to Richard Pryor as an example of a comic whose anger was taken away. "When all of a sudden you have everything you want, it's real hard to create that anger again, 'cause it's not there. But my humor has always come from wanting to put out a careless vibe. I don't have to be angry to create."

With all the notoriety came people who merely wanted to exploit Carrey's suddenly hot status. Shortly after the release of *Ace Ventura* came news of another movie that Carrey made back in 1991 surfacing for a possible theatrical release. *High Strung* was virtually a one-man standup routine written and performed by Steve Oedekerk that Carrey agreed to appear in out of loyalty to the former *In Living Color* writer and fellow stand-up comic who went on to become a creative consultant on *Ace Ventura: Pet Detective* and to pen the sequel, *Ace Ventura: When Nature Calls.* Carrey did the movie as a favor for Oedekerk, whom he met when they worked at *In Living Color.*

The film takes place in the apartment of a neurotic named Thane, whose list of phobias includes relationships, breakfast cereals, junk mail and the fly buzzing around his apartment, among other things. The $400,000 for the movie was put up by a pair of Russian immigrants and directed by rookie Roger Nygaard. Carrey appears in the movie only in brief flashes as a mysterious, shadowy figure, with the exception of one ten-minute scene at the end. And while his contract stipulated his cameo was to be unbilled in the movie, other actors show up in small, credited parts, including Fred Willard as an insurance agent, *Back to the Future* villain Thomas F. Wilson as Thane's best friend, and *Star Trek: the Next Generation*'s Denise Crosby as his boss.

Carrey's management asked the film's distributors, Rocket Pictures, not to use Carrey's name and likeness in association with the movie, though one of the company's principals, Tom Coleman, who bought the theatrical and home video rights to the film after Carrey got hot, politely declined, indicating he would use the comic in the movie's marketing plan.

"Every superstar, from Kevin Costner and Sylvester Stallone to Arnold Schwarzenegger, had two or three pictures of terrible quality out there that people capitalized on," Coleman told reporter Daniel Cerone. "This is different. It's really a good movie. He's quite funny, and he should be proud of it. It's not like he took his clothes off or anything, like Stallone did."

"Back then, Jim wanted to secure his position, because when we were making the movie, his star was just about to bloom," said the movie's executive producer Vladimir Horunzhy, a former orchestra conductor who left Russia 15 years before with rock guitarist Sergei Zholobetsky when the two refused to join the Communist Party. Horunzhy convinced Zholobetsky to put his entire savings, earned selling medical equipment, into the movie. The picture received good notices at several film festivals, but no theatrical or home video distributor showed any interest in releasing it ... until *Ace Ventura* suddenly gave the film new life.

Still, while Carrey's contract limited the use of

his name, that didn't stop Rocket from featuring the actor in a promotional trailer and using his name and photo in their advertising campaign. Coleman stressed, however, that Rocket was abiding by their original agreement. There's even a National Radio Review saying Carrey was funnier in *High Strung* than he was in *Ace Ventura*.

It was Jim Carrey's first taste of the perils of fame. And it wouldn't be his last.

EIGHT

The Man Behind The Mask

THE success of *Ace Ventura* and the subsequent $7-million-dollar deal with New Line thrust Jim Carrey into the spotlight he'd always craved. The star and the movie were the talk of Hollywood, and the principals associated with the film were seeing their careers skyrocket. The Hollywood dreams he had on Mulholland were starting to come true and he was living the fantasy life he had always dreamed of. Without his wife and child, he embarked on a whirlwind of nonstop activity preparing for that summer's release of *The Mask*, a special effects–laden $20-million movie based on the cult comic book, which was increasingly being touted by the expectant press as the year's sleeper . . . and further proof of Carrey's star power.

New Line's 28-year-old wunderkind President of Production Mike De Luca defended his company's investment in the film, which was the largest budgeted in its history. The company had previously been known mainly for the *Nightmare On Elm Street* and the *Mutant Ninja Turtle* series. He insisted to *GQ* that people "want to laugh more than they want to be educated . . . [They] want to escape their shitty lives, [not] have their faces rubbed in it." He concluded by saying the best part of the film business was the fact there was room for both an *Ace Ventura* and a *Schindler's List*.

Flushed with the success of *Ace* and the promise of a $7-million payday, Carrey grabbed his old pal songwriter Phil Roy and took a trip to Europe. The pair landed in Paris and walked into a shop to indulge Roy's love of 18th century prints and etchings. While there, the pair spotted an amazingly large, intricate painting, made up of sixteen panels depicting heaven and hell. Phil bought the piece and had it shipped back to Los Angeles. When they got back and the artwork arrived, Carrey held it up against the wall to see where to hang it.

"I couldn't see the top half, so I told him to

'move heaven down here,' " recalls Roy.

"Jim turned to me and immediately went, 'You missed one. That would make a great song title.' Because he knew I was always analyzing conversations for possible lyrics."

Roy returned with a piece of music he had composed with the help of two frequent collaborators, Rick Neigher, who has written for Joe Cocker and John Shanks, Melissa Etheridge's guitarist. "We pieced together the melody for the song that day," says Phil. "I had this wonderful tune, but I didn't know what it was called yet. So I played it for Jim and he said, 'That's it. That's "Heaven Down Here." ' He came up with the melody hook, 'Let's bring heaven down here.' And then we spent about three weeks on the lyric. We really took a lot of time and care in making sure it was perfect. I'm very proud of that song. It was amazing that this painting, after a couple of hundred years, is still inspiring people to write and make art. It's an incredible piece of work."

It wasn't until the following year that a pal of Roy's, an A&R executive at Epic Records would send the song to New Age jazz duo Tuck & Patti, who picked it out from literally hundreds of choices to be on their album, "Learning How to Fly."

"We heard the song and I said, 'I have to have it,' " recalls vocalist Patti Cathcart. "Then I found out Jim Carrey was responsible for the idea—and who would have thought, after seeing Jim's movies, that he would come up with such sweet, romantic subject matter?"

Indeed, the soaring, starkly romantic ballad, in which Cathcart wraps her sensuous voice around the yearning lyrics, backed only by a gently plucked acoustic guitar, show that Carrey was indeed starting to experience heavenly bliss rather than the fiery demons of hell he'd come through.

"I don't want to wait for the angels / Let's bring heaven down here" is the melodic chorus hook that was Carrey's creation and he received one-fourth credit for the song with Roy, Neigher, and Shanks.

And while most people could not equate the earnest romanticism of "Heaven Down Here" with his goofy on-screen persona, old pal Roy knew better.

"He's a serious guy. I mean, sure you see him in the movies and in his act. But if you go out and have dinner with him, you're going to have a great time. But he's also a very serious, sensitive, introspective man. You just can't be on like that all the time. I don't think anyone would expect him to. That's a real side of Jim. If you listen to the song, he's an important part of it."

"It's so romantic," Carrey said of the song. "Be careful who you play it for, 'cause you'll never get rid of them."

"The song is one of my favorite cuts," says Roy. "And of all the singers who've performed my songs, Tuck & Patti's version of this song is my favorite. They really took it and made it their own. I completely love what they did with it. When we heard they were doing the song, Jim was a little disappointed. 'Tuck & Patti?' But we both think they did an incredible job. They sent us a rough of it, we were blown away. Jim was like, 'Wow! Listen to our song!' I mean, Tuck & Patti are serious artists.

"I mean, is the song beautiful or what? So many people are afraid to be beautiful these days. And there's nothing wrong with it. There's nothing wrong with beauty at any point in your life."

To make just that point, Tuck & Patti's album was released on Valentine's Day 1995.

Roy went on to place a song on *The Mask* soundtrack, Domino's version of "This Business of Love." *The Mask*, of course, would spotlight Carrey's abilities as both a singer and dancer with a couple of dazzlingly choreographed set pieces.

"He's good. He can sing," insists Roy. "Jim and I have written about six songs together. If anyone out there wants a blues song, we've got a great one for you. 'Mark Twain Blues.' I've written one blues in my entire career. We wrote this one while sitting in the Daily Grill at 7 o'clock one night."

In early June, right after he had begun filming *Dumb and Dumber* in Utah and before he was to go to Cannes to promote *The Mask*, Carrey had gall bladder surgery. His old pal from his Toronto club days, Wayne Flemming, was by his side in Atlanta the day *Ace Ventura* opened, recalled a heavily sedated Carrey trying to stick-shift the gurney and drive it (shades of the scene in *Earth Girls Are Easy*), making "brrrrm-brrmm" noises with his mouth. "Y'know we have a secret handshake," said Wayne. "I'm 46 and he's 32, and people are looking at us, like, 'Excuse me, are you two adults?' No, we're not. We never claimed to be. . . ."

After that, it was off to Cannes, where Carrey reveled in his role as movie star. Staying at a hotel on the Croisette, Carrey does interviews all day on the beach, keeping the atmosphere lively by tossing beach umbrellas around, digging sand between his legs doggy-style, and grabbing an E! Entertainment light reflector and insisting it is Liz Taylor's diaphragm. To top it all off, while he's in his room, he gets a phone call from his assistant, Linda Fields, telling him Robin Williams has dropped out of the running for the much-coveted Riddler role in the next Batman movie. Director Joel Schumacher wants Carrey and they're willing to ante up $5 million to get him.

When Carrey hears the news, he's visibly stunned and reaches for a chair to hold himself up. "I feel like Eugene," he tells Linda. "I feel like fucking Eugene—Eugene in fucking Cannes."

It's a reference to the middle name he always hated as a kid but learned to cherish as the side which keeps him honest. Which keeps his feet on the ground. Because there's always a yin for that yang, a life check to be paid, a hell for every heaven . . .

"I call it the Eugene syndrome," he told a Hollywood reporter. "I always figured my parents named me that to keep me humble. You can never get too cool with a name like Eugene."

Back at the beach, the nonstop media circus begins to take its toll on Jim, who turns to his agent, Nick Stevens and says the place is making him nervous.

"I'd imagine so," Nick answered. "People poking at you all the time."

"It's not a natural state of affairs," says Jim, taking a hit on his omnipresent Marlboro Lights.

The pressure of the previous six months was getting to Carrey. One of the decisions facing him was whether to return to *In Living Color* for a sixth season. With offers piling in, it was beginning to look impossible, but he still had loyalty to the show that gave him his big boost.

He told the *L.A. Times* he was scheduled to go back, but wasn't sure yet because of the promise of things he "would love" to do. Carrey vowed, if he did return, he'd give it his best shot because it was the show that got him started, but he was already wavering. "I don't want to screw those guys. It just gets, like, you just do what you can."

The decision was made for Carrey when the show was canceled not long afterwards. "It is unbelievable timing," he marveled to the *L.A. Daily News*. "I don't know who's guiding all this, but it just seems so perfect, the way it's all falling into place."

His love life was also starting to fall into place as he became involved in a romance with co-star Lauren Holly of *Picket Fences* fame on the Utah set of *Dumb and Dumber* that spring. Since the break-up of his marriage the summer before, Carrey had hardly even had a chance to date, let alone start a relationship.

He told about going out with a girl right before *Ace Ventura* came out, but when they went for a ride on L.A.'s Hollywood Freeway in his black Lexus, when she hauled back and punched him, thinking he'd like it. Marveled Carrey: "I guess people think I'm a lot weirder than I am."

Anyway, the first clue that Carrey and Holly were an item came when the crew noticed the two stars' director's chairs kept getting closer and closer together day by day. The two then filmed a seminude love scene described as "heartfelt" by an observer in *People* magazine.

A squirt-gun fight and several furtive moments holding hands clinched the matter.

"They were lovebirds, in a world of their own," said ex-SNL'er and *Dumb and Dumber* co-star Charles Rocket.

"I know it sounds cliché," said Carrey. "Everybody goes, 'Oh gosh, the leading lady and the leading man.' But if you're making movies, that's where you meet people."

"Lauren is full of vim and vigor," said Rocket. "Like Jim, she is very open and friendly. They're perfectly matched that way."

And their personal lives had come unraveled at about the same time. Holly filed for divorce in October '93 after two-and-a-half years of marriage to Anthony Quinn's son, actor Danny Quinn, who starred in the straight-to-video movie, *Scanner Cop*. Carrey, of course, had officially ended his seven-year marriage to Melissa Womer in November, but the two were still wrangling in court over the reported $25,300 a month in child and spousal support he was paying her.

"Creative people just don't behave well generally. I mean, when my marriage was falling apart, I started looking around for examples of solid relationships. I'd go, 'Look at Tom Cruise—he's handled the movie-star thing and the marriage thing pretty solidly.' Then someone would point out that he divorced Mimi Rogers. My point is, if you're looking for examples of good behavior in show business, you're gonna get depressed real fast."

The tabloids were rampant with reports that Carrey was giving his ex-wife a hard time in terms of what he was willing to pay in alimony, but it was clear Jim was spending his newfound fortune.

"The money and stuff is a wonderful thing," he admitted to *People*. "I spend it."

128

Indeed, he had bought a 1965 robin's egg–blue Thunderbird and what was reported by the *L.A. Times* as a $4 million-dollar home in Brentwood "about a mile and a half from the bloody glove," he joked, with two master suites, chauffeur's quarters, a tennis court, a pool, two spas, a lagoon, a wading pool, a waterfall, and pool house with a big-screen TV and sauna. The house was on an acre of land, behind gates with canyon views. There were seven bedrooms in the 11,000-square-foot mansion, which was built in the '50s but gutted and rehabbed in 1990. The home had been on the market for a few years, at first in the $6 million range and finally at an asking price of $4.4 million.

"He's such a true Canadian, he's going to take out the net from the center of the tennis court and put nets on either end so we can play ball hockey," said pal Wayne Flemming.

The rest of his money was earmarked for his daughter's college education. But not a diamond engagement ring. Not yet. After being married for seven years and having gone through a bitter divorce, he wasn't about to commit to another relationship for a while.

The Mask opened around the country on July 29, 1994. The movie centers on the character of Stanley Ipkiss, a meek, lovelorn bank teller whom we first meet as he's offering tickets to a hot concert to a fellow worker in the hopes of getting a date, only to end up giving the pair away when his quarry insists she can't go without her girlfriend. Like Carrey himself, Ipkiss is an ordinary guy thrust into extraordinary circumstances when he discovers a libidinous, wish-fulfilling alter ego that must be let loose. In the movie, it's an ancient Norse mask that causes the transformation; for Carrey, it was the power of the big screen itself.

"My crotch on the big screen is about ten feet long," he enthused to MTV when Chris Connelly asked him what he liked best about his acting in *The Mask*.

The film itself was based on the cult Dark Horse Comics series about a guy who uses supernatural powers given to him by a mask to fight crime. In Jim Carrey's hands, Ipkiss discovers the mask floating in the ocean as he stands on a bridge at the nadir of his existence—he can't get a date, he gets no respect from anyone around him, and his broken-down Studebaker has just died. It is a scene reminiscent of both *It's a Wonderful Life* with his beloved Jimmy Stewart and his own experiences on Mulholland Drive contemplating the lights of an elusive Hollywood stardom. In keeping with Jim's humanistic bent, he only jumps in the water because he thinks the mask is someone who's drowning. When he finally picks it up, he's ready to chalk it up as one more bummer on a day full of them, but as a cop asks what he's doing down there, Carrey replies, "I was looking for my mask . . . and I found it!!" He may as well have been announcing his arrival as a movie star, because that is the true moment that Jim Carrey becomes the Seven-to-Ten-Million-Dollar Man.

Once Carrey puts on the mask and enters the screen fiction, all boundaries between time and space are off, anything is possible . . . thanks to Carrey's rubberized features and Industrial Light & Magic. Carrey can then begin to live out his most id-busting fantasies as he sets his sights on bodacious newcomer Cameron Diaz, a sizzling 21-year-old model-turned-actress from Long Beach, California, with a body that *The New York Times* insisted "makes Anna Nicole Smith look like a feminist college professor." It's almost as if art had imitated life, with Carrey donning the mask of Jim Carrey Movie Star in real life, where his every wish, no matter how lascivious, is granted.

Carrey admitted he found it funny to portray a very weird guy who thinks he's totally cool. "That sort of demented, completely unjustified confidence is very likable, but it also makes you laugh," he told *Entertainment Weekly*, adding *The Mask* and *Ace* were both like that, "but very different, too." One of the differences was, for *Ace*, he only had to show up on the set in Hawaiian shirt and sneakers, while for *The Mask*, he needed almost four hours to put on the elaborate make-up and prosthetics before filming could begin.

Indeed, Carrey's makeup was designed by Academy Award-winner Greg Cannom, who fashioned a series of latex pieces that would allow Jim's natural facial expressions to come through.

"Jim Carrey is so funny, burying his facial movements under latex would be a crime," said the movie's director, Charles Russell, whose previous experience had come on New Line's *Nightmare on Elm Street 3* as well as a remake of *The Blob*. "The makeup ensured that when Jim moved his eyebrows or changed his expression, it wouldn't be lost."

Indeed, when Carrey had first visited George Lucas's Industrial Light & Magic in Marin, California, before filming began in order to meet the special effects pros that provided much of the film's dazzling visuals, he said, "I went up there for some photo tests and all these guys who had just done *Jurassic Park* and *Terminator 2* were standing around. So I started going crazy, y'know, doing my thing and at the end they came up to me and said, 'What the hell do you need us for?' "

"The beauty of Jim Carrey is that he can go pretty far, but there are things even he doesn't have the ability to do," said Industrial Light & Magic's Clint Goldman. "So, he goes as far as he can, and then we can take it that much further. For example, Jim Carrey can do weird and wild things with his mouth, but he can't take his jaw and drop it all the way down to the ground or have it tongue roll out on the table."

With the help of the makeup, though, Jim admitted a metamorphosis took place. "As soon as I was made up, I became 'The Mask.' I could feel the character just burst through me. Basically, it was a joygasm and that's what the movie is, pure adrenaline."

The character encapsulated Carrey's own yin-yang, heaven-hell balancing act. "On one level, I'm this sweet, innocent guy, and on another level, I'm this wound-up ball of spontaneous combustion."

The movie pays homage to the surreal speed and grace of animation pioneer Tex Avery, who directed cartoons at Warner Bros., where he helped create Bugs Bunny and Daffy Duck, but hit his peak at MGM, where he created 65 classic cartoons from 1942 to 1955 starring Droopy, a rather "dyspeptic" dog. The scene where Carrey spots Cameron Diaz's sultry Tina Carlyle doing her act on the stage of the Coco Bongo nightclub—as his eyeballs bulge from their sockets, his heart pounds outside his chest, his tongue unravels like a red carpet, and he turns into a wolf, howling at the moon, then slamming himself over the head with a mallet to calm down— is based on Avery's '43 cartoon *Red Hot Riding Hood*, which also served as an inspiration for *Who Framed Roger Rabbit?* To drive the point home, Carrey as Ipkiss is shown laughing along with the same cartoon on video in his apartment right before he dons the mask for the first time.

Instead of being overshadowed by the special effects, Carrey is transformed into a larger-than-life version of himself. With his green makeup, mouth full of platinum piano-key teeth, and a leering grin, it is impossible to tell where the human ends and the morphing begins, which is exactly what Carrey and director Russell had intended.

"Jim is an amazing athlete," says Russell. "What he does with his body reminds me of the old silent-film star, Harold Lloyd. The guys from

Industrial Light & Magic told me that we saved a million dollars in optical effects because of the things that Jim does for real."

"Nobody does what Jim does," added New Line's Mike De Luca. "He's got that uncanny ability to be Everyman and a crazy man. I haven't seen anything like that since Eddie Murphy first hit the screen."

The Mask was shot entirely in Los Angeles, with Carrey shuttling between the movie's sets and his gig at *In Living Color*. Production designer Craig Stearns utilized historic L.A. locations and customized them to give Edge City, the fictional metropolis where the movie takes place, its unique urban identity. The Edge City Bank, where Ipkiss works, was in reality an old Bank of America building in downtown Los Angeles, replete with polished marble floors, high gold-leafed ceilings and arched doorways. The bank was filled with modern furniture, which purposely blurred the time frame.

Like Ace Ventura, Carrey's Stanley Ipkiss inhabits his own insular, circumscribed world. Like Ventura, he has a way with animals, in this case a charismatic, frisbee-catching Jack Russell terrier named Milo. His apartment is furnished in "thrift shop chic," filled with cartoon figure lamps, Porky Pig and Daffy Duck animation cels, animated videos, comic books and toys.

There is a poignancy to the pre-Mask scenes, a sweet melancholy that shows Jim Carrey's potential as a leading man.

Raved New Line's De Luca: "There's a whole other side to Jim Carrey in this film. I'm not kidding you when I say he reminds me of a young Jimmy Stewart in *Mr. Smith Goes to Washington*."

Not coincidentally, one of Carrey's favorite movies.

Director Russell, who originally screen-tested Jim for a part when he directed the 1986 Rodney Dangerfield comedy, *Back To School*, told the *L.A. Daily News*: "I'd never seen anything like the comic energy this guy had and I never forgot him. Frankly, I'm the least-surprised guy in Hollywood that he's become a star. He takes his stuff to a dangerous edge, which takes courage and imagination and which audiences appreciate. And he's lovable. That's actually the definition of any leading man: a sense of danger and some charm. Jim has those qualities and a very brilliant comic wit."

That wit came into effect the moment Carrey's Ipkiss donned the ancient Nordic relic and transformed himself into the banana yellow, zoot-suited (a nod to the polyester suit his mom made him wear to Yuk-Yuk's), finger-snappin' mojo man. "Sssssssmokin'," he says, once again invoking the Carrey fascination with fire. Before he sets out for the Coco Bongo to find Tina, he preens for the camera and hisses: "Hold on, sugar daddy's got a sweet tooth tonight! S-s-s-somebody stop me!"

And then he proceeds to literally bounce off the walls, duck bullets, and smash a runaway alarm clock with a large hammer before terrorizing his apartment manager. Landlords give Ace Ventura and Stanley Ipkiss a hard time while the gas company drives *Dumb and Dumber*'s Lloyd Christmas and his roommate / best friend Harry into the street.

Riffing on his new persona, Carrey gets to rummage through several of his filmic references, including Elvis Presley, W.C. Fields, Clark Gable, Edward G. Robinson, Desi Arnaz, Andy Devine, Sally Field at the Oscars ("You like me, you really like me"), Clint Eastwood as "Dirty Harry" ("Well, do you feel lucky . . . punk?), and the guy in the commercial who exclaimed, "That's a spicy meatball!," the latter after swallowing a bomb and burping fire. Not to mention such purely fictional creations as a dying cowboy, a French apache dancer, a carnival barker, a southern preacher, a boy and his dog, and Bob Crachitt of *A Christmas Carol*. Jim also gets to show off his "Fred Astaire-on-acid" moves in a pair of lavishly choreographed dance sequences, one of which takes place at the fictional night club Coco Bongo, which was filmed at the historic Park Plaza Hotel in L.A.'s mid-Wilshire district, filled with palm trees and a running waterfall awash in violet spotlights to make it look like a fantasy dance hall that would be equally at place in the '40s or the 21st century. Deco light fixtures and a tiered stage with lit steps completed the scene.

The house band at the Coco Bongo was played by the Royal Crown Revue, whose own "Hey Pachuco" was used for the initial dance scene with Carrey and Diaz. Director Russell heard a tape of the song from a friend of his and immediately knew this was the kind of musical outfit he wanted for the scene. The L.A.–based group played authentic big band music faithfully, down to their '40s suits and swing rhythms, holding down a regular weekly gig at the new Brown Derby nightclub in Los Feliz, where they attracted a hip, young Hollywood crowd.

"He saw the vibe of the band and thought it would be great to use the song for the scene he had in mind," said the band's Scott Steen, who gets the major Cecil B. DeMille close-up as he gets to sing out the title line. The elaborate scene, including the incredible pas de deux with Carrey and Diaz which was nominated for an MTV Movie Award as one of the year's "Best Dance Sequences," took almost two weeks to film.

"He had rehearsed with a dancing coach for that scene before he ever came in," said Steen. "When we came in, he was more or less ready to go. We were on the set with him for a week and a half . . . ten, twelve hours a day. The one thing I noticed about Jim the most is, he'd be real entertaining, screw around and have a real good time while acting the class clown, but only when he wasn't working. The moment it came time for him to step up, he'd immediately switch gears. He was real professional. But a total cut-up from the moment they said, 'Cut,' to when they said, 'Rolling.' Jim was very entertaining. And he wasn't even trying. He's just naturally funny. And a pretty relaxed guy. When he's one-on-one just sitting down with you, he gets more comfortable. When he was moving in between takes, he could get pretty energetic. But he always stayed focused. One thing I noticed about Jim is, he's always thinking, but he isn't uptight about it. It's so fluid, almost like a casual intensity. He's real confident in what he does."

The initial dance sequence in the Coco Bongo

is amazing in the way it combines Carrey's incredible dexterity and almost rubber legs with the computerized special effects into a seamless whole. Between takes, director Russell allowed the band to jam, and Carrey showed a special interest.

"He talked to us about the band, about jazz," says Steen. "We told him a little about us, how we got together. He was curious how a young bunch of guys like us could end up playing traditional music like this. We talked a little bit about jazz, some straight-ahead stuff. He's really diverse in his musical tastes; he just appreciates good music. He checked us out pretty intently when we played on the set. Jim's got some real musical talent."

"He told me he's into Toad the Wet Sprocket," said his good buddy Phil Roy. "He's been into everything from Jackie Wilson to Pantera. Oh, yeah. He likes Tom Petty, too. His tastes probably run more on the metal side than the R&B side, though."

Carrey's good humor was a welcome element on the set of *The Mask*.

"You know how they say about certain actors that they make all the actors around them feel better?" asked comic Richard Jeni, who costarred in the movie. "Well, Jim makes all the other actors feel normal. No matter what's going on around him—it could be a plane wreck—he'll walk up to you and go, 'A-ha-ha!' That's something you wouldn't get if you were working with Mickey Rourke or Meryl Streep. They would not work like that."

Steen also had a tale about Carrey's mischievousness on the set, undoubtedly inspired by the elfin character he was portraying.

"We'd been on the set for about twelve hours, gigged that night, then came back at 7 the next morning. I was sitting on the stairs of the Park View, where we filmed the Coco Bongo stuff, falling asleep. All of a sudden, I felt something strange, woke up and had this big green mask staring me in the face and people are laughing. It was him with his face about an inch from mine hanging down from the top of the stairs. I was startled. It was real weird to look up and see that big green face there like that. The point is, he didn't put himself on a higher level than anybody else. We all had a good time."

Carrey's second tour de force set-piece comes with "Cuban Pete," which he sings himself in an outrageous Zorro hat, ruffled shirt, and flamenco pants, turning a manhunt into a musical number, spoofing the Ricky Ricardo-type he often played on *In Living Color*. As the police spotlights shine on him, he hops up on the hood of a squad car and leads the assembled masses in a demented rumba line. To add to the effect, Carrey's costumes were completely over-the-top in both bright, primary colors and design, helping him get into *The Mask*'s manic character for each scene. Costume designer Ha Nguyen used highly stylized wardrobes to bring out each new transformation for Carrey.

"Because the character of *The Mask* is so vibrant, I purposely dressed everyone else in more subdued colors," she says in the film's production notes. "I wanted him to leap off the screen whenever he appears, so his palette is entirely exaggerated colors, like canary yellow and bright turquoise." Both Nguyen and production designer Stearns give little clues to the panache of *The Mask* in Stanley Ipkiss' pre-transformation wardrobe, which becomes a key plot element in the film.

"I tried to pick up the pattern in his apartment and translate it into his ties," explains Nguyen.

If New Line was at all nervous about the $7 million they had plunked down for Carrey to star in *Dumb and Dumber*, their fears had to be alleviated by the $24.9 million *The Mask* generated at the box office in its opening weekend, on the way to $120 million in the U.S. and over $300 million worldwide in grosses. Carrey was a star and *The Mask* reviews, unlike the beating *Ace Ventura* took, acknowledged the budding phenomenon.

"Call him jerkier than Jerry Lewis, geekier than Jim Varney, and more manic than Robin Williams," wrote *Rolling Stone*'s Peter Travers. "You can't beat Carrey . . . *The Mask* is the summer's funniest movie . . . [with] a flair for mischief that is uniquely Carrey's . . .

"Carrey is a comic fireball in a tour de force display of physical antics that should convert his most rabid detractors. . . . Those who believe nothing short of Prozac can slow Carrey down will welcome his sweetness with Diaz as Stanley tries to express his feelings for Tina without relying on the mask. . . .

"But the crowds won't flock to *The Mask* for subtlety. they want to see Carrey play monkey boy and go bananas. That he does, especially in a free-for-all climax that pulls out all the stops in head-spinning hilarity. Even when the gags are labored, Carrey stays light on his feet. This gifted clown has found the right vehicle for his souped-up silliness. Carrey is the ultimate party dude, and like the masked man says, this party is smokin'."

The New York Times' Janet Maislin dismissed

the movie as an example of "the shrinking importance of conventional storytelling in special effects–minded movies," but praised Carrey as "bright-eyed, crazily intense, irrepressibly silly . . . Mr. Carrey can be funny without fireworks. He deserves material clever enough to let him do just that."

Maislin did realize "if you build a film this way, as Hollywood continues to discover, they—the audiences—will come."

For Jim Carrey, *The Mask* turned out to be a potent metaphor for his own rise to superstardom. It was becoming increasingly impossible for him to reveal the person underneath the larger-than-life celebrityhood, the normal, regular guy who only wanted to be loved for himself—one of the movie's chief messages.

"Although it was sheer hell putting on the mask every day for four hours, it was so liberating as an actor," Carrey told *The Orange County Register*. "As actors we put on masks all the time by assuming our character's identity, but then to be able to put on a mask on top of that mask was exhilarating.

"But I also liked the metaphor inherent in the movie. There is a definite message in there about the masks we all put on every day. Everybody wants to be perceived as being so cool that they're untouched by life. Everybody wants to be perceived as Mr. Winner. I'm no different than anyone else in that respect."

NINE

Jim Carrey's Divine Ignorance: "Dumb is as Dumb Does"

IT may have taken him years of therapy and self-analysis—from ribbon auras to colonics to shrinks—but Jim Carrey eventually recognized there was a theme running through many of his characters—guys who think they're in control, but aren't.

"Anybody who says they are is full of shit," he said.

With the success of both *Ace Ventura* and *The Mask* and his subsequent split with his wife, Jim Carrey was anything but in control, but he was also having a hell of a good time. Stardom did have its down sides, though, including a complete lack of privacy. He was finding it impossible to leave his new $4-million mansion without being asked to do one of his patented routines by fawning fans.

"Usually, I comply, though occasionally I want to be left alone," Carrey told *US* magazine. "That's when they start asking, 'What's the matter, man, don't you like your job?' I say: 'Yeah, I like my job. But I also like fucking. And I'm not gonna do that in front of you, either.

"It's insane, it really is. People come over to my house and say, 'Hey, I have this friend who has a script you should read' and I just take them over to the cupboard and there's literally 50 scripts in there that I need to attend to at some point. It's impossible."

And while *Ace Ventura* was now climbing to the top of the home video charts, and the summer hit *The Mask* was still selling tickets, *Dumb and Dumber* came out in theaters nationwide on December 16, 1994, with an ad campaign which mocked the summer's big film, *Forrest Gump*, by proclaiming, "Dumb happens." Coincidentally, both movies are about the redeeming powers of ignorance and simple-mindedness, something most film critics duly noted with no small measure of disdain.

"The poster is funnier than anything in the movie," wrote *Rolling Stone*, though Carrey fan Peter Travers went out of his way to note, "[he is] a genuine comic talent even when mired in drivel . . . a monkey boy for the ages."

The notion of a thin veneer of control which keeps civilization from falling apart has been a recurrent theme in Carrey's life and work since the days when his father lost his job and his own family was thrown into turmoil. *Dumb and Dumber* continues to explore people who ignore their own desperate circumstances because, well, they're oblivious to how bad off they really are.

How dumb are they? Well, at one point Lloyd solemnly informs Harry that the Monkees were the biggest influence on the Beatles. Later in the movie, glancing at a 1969 poster of the Moon Landing, Lloyd's mouth opens in astonishment as he exclaims: "Hey, no way! That's great!" These guys make Forrest Gump look like Einstein.

"The movie is about two of the dumbest guys in the history of the world going on a road trip, who do some of the dumbest things known to man . . . and live to tell about it," according to co-star Jeff Daniels, who was actually Jim Carrey's personal pick to play his sidekick Harry Dunne.

Carrey, who had casting approval, had an instant rapport with Daniels. "It was like communication, rather than two separate clowns going at it. So I fought for him. But it wasn't quite what the marketing geniuses had in mind. They wanted someone with an MTV profile, whatever that means." Consider yourself lucky *Dumb and Dumber* didn't star Pauly Shore and Kennedy.

"It was perfect casting," insists Daniels. "They decided they needed an actor who wasn't too bright. Bingo!! Anyway, I needed to be stupid for awhile."

Carrey created a whole new character in Lloyd Christmas, who actually made both Ace Ventura and Stanley Ipkiss seem like Mensa candidates. Jim opted to go against the romantic lead his manager and agent probably hoped for and went completely in the other direction, creating one of the biggest nerds in the history of cinema, with a pudding-bowl haircut modeled after Jerry Lewis in *Geisha Boy*.

To get his dumb look just right, Carrey combined Spock from *Star Trek*, an ancient monk and Jerry Lewis in *The Nutty Professor*. "The short bangs seem to do it nicely. I also figured now would be the best time to reveal my chipped tooth," he said of an old injury which came from the time his best friend did a running cannonball leap onto his head while he was resting it on a desk at school. "I thought the tooth looked cool until I turned 13 and my penis said to me, 'You might want to get that fixed, Jim.' "

Carrey vowed not to let his $7-million status affect his characterization, either.

"This is where people get safe and do the toe-the-line type thing," he told MTV. "And I thought, this is where I take that leading man thing they're expecting and turn it inside out. So I had this character with a chipped tooth like he smashed himself in the face with a ball-peen hammer and they loved it."

The movie was written by the brother team of Peter and Bob Farrelly along with Bennett Yellin, as Peter made his film directing debut. The Cumberland, Rhode Island native had previously written numerous comedies for television, including an NBC special with Jay Leno and the Zucker Brothers of *Airplane* fame, an HBO special with Paul Reiser and a pair of episodes for *Seinfeld*. The script was originally sent to Carrey while he was shooting *The Mask* and he fell in love with it, immediately going to work with the writers to help fine-tune the script.

"We just kept pecking away, making it funnier and funnier and funnier," he said. "Even though Lloyd and Harry have screwed-up morals, we wanted to help bring out their innocence since there is a wholesale purity about them."

From the very start of production in Breckenridge, Colorado, Carrey and Daniels sought to stretch stupidity to its outer limit.

"Jeff followed Jim's lead," said producer Charles Wessler. "Like a great dancer would follow a lead. They worked very well off each other."

There were often last-minute improvisations which made the movie even better.

"The script changed every day," says Daniels. "We'd walk on the set and Peter would ask, 'Is there anything extra we can do here?' and of course Jim, who only needs a little crack in the door, would be ready with a whole bunch of ideas. So ten minutes before we shot, we'd make changes that worked really well, and we went with them."

One of those scenes is in the diner, where Carrey and Daniels crack up as Jim calls the waitress "Flo," then asks seriously, "What's the soup du jour?" and when she responds, "It's the soup of the day," he grins vacantly and nods, "That sounds good." When MTV's Chris Connelly asked Carrey if it were an ad-lib, he claimed not to know what he was talking about.

"I'm just with the program," he insisted. "I show up, do the work, it's over. I don't want to hang with that." Meaning, he works in the moment and then it's on to the next thing, not looking back for an instant.

The comic timing between the two is exquisite in the manner of classic teams like Abbott & Costello, Laurel & Hardy, Beavis & Butt-head, or Hope & Crosby. It would be a shame if Carrey & Daniels didn't make more comedies together in the future.

"I really wanted to work with Jim," says Daniels. "He's obviously very hot right now, but he's also very talented. Working with someone as good at comedy as Jim is was certainly a challenge. His mind works at a whole different speed."

Carrey on Daniels: "This is definitely the role he was born to play. He's tapped into something that I think is going to be his trademark for the rest of time. This is him, this is really it.

"Seriously, he's a wonderful actor, and my favorite from the start. The idea that I could play this wild character and work with an actor that I could learn something from was great. It's really fun to watch someone like Jeff totally let go. We had a great time."

Director Farrelly also learned something while working with Carrey. Don't yell cut until you're sure the scene is over, realizing some of the actor's best stuff came at those moments.

Added producer Wessler: "Jim Carrey is not playing the same note every time... What he does as an actor is incredibly unique."

So who was dumb... and who dumber?

"It's a horse race," says Daniels. "I think every time Jim is dumb, I'm dumber. Then we cut back to Jim who does or says something even dumber. And this goes on and on...."

To prepare for their roles, both actors underwent "dumbness" preparation. Says Carrey: "When the cameras roll, we just get the glassy, 'I-just-ate-lead-paint-for-breakfast' look. We don't gear up for it. We gear down."

Daniels adds: "You basically empty your head. You go blank. You try to get the I.Q. down as close to zero as possible and still make the characters believable. If people see this movie and can think of anyone who is dumber than we are, then we haven't done our job."

Lloyd Christmas is, like many of Carrey's characters, a hopeless romantic. He will do anything for the one he loves, and he just happens to fixate on Lauren Holly's Mary Swanson when, as a chauffeur, he picks her up to take her to the airport. "Where are you going?" he asks. "Aspen," she answers. "Mmmmm, California, nice," he deadpans obliviously before causing a gas tank to go up in flames because he's not watching where he's driving.

The series of mishaps echoes the "Eugene Factor" in Carrey's own life.

"My life is a string of embarrassing moments," he says. "I've gone to premieres and tried to make the cool-guy exit, and the limo driver locks the keys in the car, and it's running, and he's trying to pick the lock while I'm standing there and the whole theater is emptying out."

Upon dropping Holly off at the airport in the movie, Carrey insists on an uncomfortably long good-bye hug, then keeps an eye on his quarry as she leaves her briefcase behind ... causing him to bang into the car in front of him and set off the airbag. A wonderful piece of physical comedy follows as Carrey struggles to get out of the car to scoop up the luggage she inadvertently left. It turns out the attaché case is filled with money and Carrey finds himself in the middle of a foiled kidnapping ransom scenario and what passes for the plot is set on its merry way.

As with all Carrey movies, though, the story is merely an excuse to string along a variety of individual sight gags and set-pieces. And while Barbara Walters insisted that "action speaks louder than words" and "talk is cheap" in Jim Carrey movies, there are some pretty good lines in *Dumb and Dumber*. And, to show off his generosity as an actor, Carrey lets Jeff Daniels have several of them.

One of the best is when the cop tries to get them to "pull over," Daniels reponds, "It's a cardigan, but thanks for noticing." And when he first meets Lauren Holly at the Endangered Species Benefit, he chirps, "Nice hooters," only to reveal he's talking about the rare owls on display.

The Carrey and Daniels characters are in desperate straits when the movie begins, in many ways echoing the position Jim found himself in before his recent spate of successes. Each has lost their job, Carrey as a chauffeur ("They always freak out when you leave the scene of an accident") and Daniels as a dog groomer (he had turned his entire car into a furry sheepdog, with headlights as eyes, and the legend "Mutt Cutts" emblazoned on the side).

Alone in their unfurnished Providence, Rhode Island, dump, Carrey looks out the window and suddenly grows wistful: "I don't want to be a nobody all my life. I want to be somebody." And the two set out for Aspen in search of romance and adventure, a buddy-buddy road movie, with the buddies sharing a single brain. Along the way, there are wonderfully mean-spirited, politically incorrect gags about little old ladies in wheelchairs stealing all their money, selling a decapitated parakeet to a blind, handicapped boy, and killing a crook with a gastric problem by sneaking hot peppers onto his hamburger, then feeding him the rat poison that was meant for them, thinking it was his prescription medicine.

If Carrey and Daniels were mainly two morons, there wouldn't be much of a movie. The genius of the pairing is the way the two bring a kind of everyman humanity to their roles, making it believable that you would stick your tongue to a frozen ski lift or kill a nearly extinct owl with a popped champagne cork.

The love scenes between Carrey and Holly resonate with the real-life, off-screen romance that was blossoming on the film's sets in Colorado, Utah, and Providence.

"They're like a couple of kids at the beginning of a relationship," said co-star Charles Rocket. "Goofing around, laughing at each other's jokes. It's a good thing these two people met. This one seems like the real deal."

Once again, Carrey concocts a wish-fulfillment fantasy scene in which he smothers Lauren's mouth in a lip lock that was nominated by MTV for one of 1994's "Best Screen Kisses."

"It's one of the best on-screen kisses," says Holly. "You've got to admit."

There's also a poignance to the scene in which Carrey's Lloyd Christmas confesses, "I like you a lot" to Holly.

"What do you think the chances are of a guy like you and a girl like me ending up together?" he asks earnestly, mixing up their sexes.

"Not good" is Holly's frank response.

"You mean not good like one in a hundred?" he says hopefully.

"I'd say more like one out of a million," she answers.

"So you're telling me there's a chance," he brightens. "Yeeaaah!"

A few moments later, when Carrey finds out she has a husband, he says in disappointment, "What happened to the one in a million?"

The line resonates outside the confines of the screen, both for the ongoing romance between the two and the tremendous odds Carrey himself has overcome on his road to stardom.

In the film's final scene, when Holly is reunited with her kidnapped husband, Carrey's Lloyd Christmas briefly fantasizes taking a gun and killing him, reminiscent of his routine in the Showtime special about the voice inside your head which dictates whether you're sane or out of your mind. As Carrey joked, you could go either way just as easily, depending on the possible response your brain sends to your body.

Because, despite the toilet humor—there are ongoing jokes about bodily secretions such as snot, saliva, piss and diarrhea—there is a surprisingly sweet, pre-sexual naïveté to *Dumb and Dumber* which makes it hard to resist. Still, one longs to see how Carrey will use that vast sexual energy he has shown—one of his patented stand-up moves is a comically exaggerated in-out/in-out hip thrust—in his future on-screen film roles. Will he ever play an adult? Will he age like Jerry Lewis and become an angry old man?

"Jerry Lewis' true personality has emerged over the years, and he's an unlikable prick and it shows," says Les Fierstein, an executive producer on *In Living Color*. "But Jim has this niceness that always comes through. He has a good soul. On the other hand, Jim's more subversive than Lewis. I mean, he will take on anything."

"Every comedian wants to die with dignity," Carrey told the *Charlotte Observer*. "That's what happened to Jerry Lewis. He got serious. I saw him doing stand-up comedy recently and he's still doing that same squeaky little-boy voice. And the man's 60 years old! Man, it's time to move on. Do something that's about now.

"I was kind of worried about Dan Aykroyd for awhile, too. Doing nothing but those silly comedy ensemble things. But he's started moving into interesting character parts lately.

"I won't be Ace when I'm 50, but there'll always be moments of craziness. The best characters to me were guys played by Jimmy Stewart: sweet and lovable and fallible. When they got downhearted, people cared about them more. I think Jimmy's a good role model . . . with a little Manson thrown in."

The success of *Dumb and Dumber*—which went on to gross $120 million, giving Carrey three 1994 movies that earned a total of more than $320 million—had critics searching for the key to his success.

Typical was *Newsday's* Gene Seymour, who talked out of both sides of his mouth when he opined: "Jim Carrey's rise to the status of America's goonybird has been so meteoric that the blue meanies who chart the movie business now make it their first priority to wait for the other shoe to drop." Say what?

L.A. Weekly called *Dumb and Dumber*, "flatly directed, sloppily edited and altogether inept. And, oh yeah, I laughed my ass off . . . The movie is essentially a chance to let Carrey rip, which he does over and over and over and over again . . . [Carrey] is undeniably talented, but has yet to find a role that capitalizes on his verbal dexterity as much as his physical gifts."

The Village Voice said simply: "Sporting nothing more elaborate than a dogbowl haircut and a chipped front tooth, Carrey is Goofy, in living, breathing color."

The New York Times noted: "If critical traditions count for anything, Jim Carrey can look forward to one day being discovered by the French film establishment and canonized as the new Jerry Lewis. There are moments all through his newest movie, when the rubber-faced actor with a chipped front tooth, his hair in bangs and his cough-drop eyes ablaze with maniacal mischief, is almost a dead ringer for Mr. Lewis on one of his hyperactive jags." It's hard to tell if that's a compliment or not, but it's a sure thing Jim Carrey does not want to be hosting the Cerebral Palsy Telethon in the year 2010.

In the middle of all his success, right as *Dumb and Dumber* was about to open, Jim's father Percy passed away, but not before he had lived to see his son achieve what he had failed to do.

"My father realized I reached my goal," Jim told Barbara Walters on an interview that aired the night of the Oscars. "He saw that I had done the thing he had hoped to do and hoped his whole life for me to do. It was finality for him . . . It was great to see it. What can I say? My life is a fairy tale."

When Carrey revealed to Walters that he had put that mythic $10-million check he wrote to himself in his father's casket, the veteran newscaster had the tables turned on her and her eyes began to moisten at Jim's heartfelt tale. At any second, you felt Jim was going to bust out laughing, but it truly was an only-in-Hollywood–type ending. And it freed Jim up from even more of his demons.

Meanwhile, the tabloids were reporting that the impending divorce with his wife Melissa was getting increasingly messy, and the accounts were not favorable to the superstar, who was accused of trying to minimize the alimony to be paid to his wife and daughter.

By the beginning of 1995, Jim Carrey was the biggest comedy star in Hollywood, probably the most popular film comic since Eddie Murphy hit with the troika of *Trading Places*, *48 Hours*, and *Beverly Hills Cop*. Except Carrey did it all in one year, making an unprecedented $300-million-plus on the three films he had released in 1994. In addition, he had a pair of best-selling home videos in *Ace Ventura* and *The Mask* and $22 million worth of upcoming film gigs with *Batman Forever* and the sequels to *Ace Ventura* and *The Mask*. And, for someone who took 15 years to make it, he remained remarkably unbitter toward the industry.

He told *Entertainment Weekly* he didn't keep an "enemies" list of people who had turned him down for jobs, saying that sort of stuff can "give you cancer . . . You've got to realize coming into this business that no one's going to take a chance on you. You have to prove you have the goods . . . It's nothing personal. It's not like anyone goes out of his way to screw you. It's just that you have to be the most popular, talented guy in the room at the exact moment they need you."

Perhaps the only individual he ever criticized was David Letterman, when he told *TV Guide*: "I've had problems with his show. I was asked to audition for his show when I was in *In Living Color*. Only when *Ace Ventura* was a hit did the Letterman people think I was worthy of being on the show. Nice of them, hunh?"

But by the close of 1994, there weren't too many who didn't acknowledge what everyone else seemed to know: Jim Carrey was the toast of Hollywood and America's Favorite Fool.

He received the National Association of Theater Owner's Comedy Star of the Year honors before an audience of 3,000 at the ShowWest convention in Las Vegas. After literally licking the award twice, he proclaimed: "This has been an incredible year for me, and you guys made it possible. We both made a great deal of money together . . . that's why I'm announcing that I'm retiring from the world of feature films.

"Obviously, I have peaked and I would be a fool to try to keep up this kind of pace. This is a year when all my dreams came true . . . except for the Michelle Pfeiffer thing."

With the exhibitors' laughs ringing in his ear, he thanked the theater owners: "If it weren't for you, I'd have no creative outlet and would surely have to be institutionalized."

It was reminiscent of the time his mother asked Jim what he would do if he failed in show business. "I told her, 'I have no idea.' "

But failure was never an option for Jim Carrey.

"I don't have a trade," he said to the *Miami Herald*. "There was no choice for me. It makes you work a little harder when you don't have an exit." If it didn't happen for him, Carrey claims, "I would have become a street person."

TEN

"Rich and Richer":
Jim Carrey Goes to Gotham
City and Beyond

CARREY admitted to the Knight-Ridder Syndicate the work was the most important thing for him. "Even if I have $40 billion in the bank, if I don't feel that I did a good job that day, I'm a basket case," he said. "I'm linked to my work in a probably extremely unhealthy way."

By the beginning of 1995, Jim Carrey had achieved everything he had ever dreamed of. He was at the pinnacle of his profession. He earned a Golden Globe nomination for "Best Actor in a Comedy or Musical" and, even though he lost to *Four Weddings and a Funeral* star Hugh Grant, he put the entire awards process in perspective by clasping his hands in mock prayer as the nominees were announced, cracking up the audience

like only Carrey could. He also lost out to Tom
Hanks at the American Comedy Awards, and
while he didn't receive any Oscar consideration,
The Mask did receive an Academy Award nomination for Best Visual Effects. Carrey was
named the ideal male chaperone in the third annual MCI Spring Break survey, garnering 36% of
the vote, winning over such heartthrobs as
Keanu Reeves (10%) and Ethan Hawke (2%). *Pre-
miere* magazine's annual Top 100 Power List had
him ranked number 12, while his coattails pulled
New Line chief Bob Shaye to 18, New Line Production President Michael De Luca to 77, and his
United Talent Agent Nick Stevens to 96. The
1995 MTV Movie Awards gave him nominations
for "Best Comedic Performance" for both *The
Mask* and *Dumb and Dumber* as well as nods for
"Best Kiss" (with current amour Lauren Holly)
and "Best Dance Sequence" for his mambo with
Cameron Diaz, who was also cited for "Breakthrough Performance."

The year started with Carrey turning down a
$17-million offer from the Motion Picture Cor-
poration of America to star in *Thief of Santa Monica*, citing "creative reasons." He kept insisting
he wasn't in this "just for the money."

"The amount of money I'm getting is so ridiculous," he told *US*. "I have financial goals, but

I've never lost sleep over money—even when I was struggling."

He'd joke about changing his name to "Ka-Ching, the sound of a cash register," but was sensitive about the impression he was greedy.

Carrey insisted to Knight-Ridder when he first wrote that $10 million check to himself, it wasn't about money, but a message to himself that he had made it, he was one of the "big boys." "The only worry I have now . . . is that people will start thinking of me as a check and not as a character. I don't want . . . audiences . . . evaluating whether that last joke was worth what I'm making."

The opportunity to star in *Batman Forever*, the third installment of the popular series, whose previous two episodes had grossed more than $700 million in worldwide receipts—to work with people lilke director Joel Schumacher and stars Val Kilmer, Tommy Lee Jones, and Nicole Kidman—meant more to him than the considerable $5 million he got to play the Riddler, a role originally played on TV by the similarly rubber-faced Frank Gorshin.

He insisted he was thrilled some of the top talents in Hollywood now wanted to work with him. "Up to now, it's been, 'Well, Jim's great, but no one wants to be in a Jim Carrey movie.' That's changed now."

When Robin Williams mysteriously dropped out of the running to play the Riddler the previous spring, Jim Carrey was director Joel Schumacher's first choice for the part.

"I don't really know . . . whether there were politics behind the scenes or what," Carrey said about getting the coveted role. "Whatever it is . . . I got the part and I'm happy. There were plenty of parts I didn't get or that didn't happen for me for one reason or another and I never questioned it, because it was not meant to be."

As soon as he learned he had the part while in Cannes the previous spring, he began planning how he'd look. He fretted about getting in shape for the skintight Riddler costume, not wanting to wear a sash around his belly.

"I have this other idea, though. You know how some people cut words and shapes into their hair? I want to carve a big question mark into the top of my head, and the period of the question mark would be made from the hair on the back of my neck." He fretted about the fact his hair might not grow back in time for him to do *Ace Ventura 2* or what the judge in his divorce proceedings might think being approached by someone with a big question mark in his head. "Excuse me, your honor, I don't mean to question your judgment. . . . "

Batman Forever is a departure in several ways from the first two films in the installment. For one, Val Kilmer was chosen over Kurt Russell and Billy Baldwin to replace Michael Keaton in the bat suit.

"Val was my first and only choice," said Schumacher, who added that Keaton never struck a deal to do the film.

Ironically, someone rumor-mongered that Carrey's star presence was one of the things which drove Keaton from the film, fearing he'd be overshadowed by the colorful villains played by Jim and Tommy Lee Jones. Others insisted he couldn't get the money he wanted nor the creative control. The actor's agent denied all the speculation, insisting Keaton "looked forward to having the opportunity to play a wide variety of roles of many genres" and that "a man who has done *Beetlejuice, Mr. Mom* and *Clean and Sober* . . . is not a man who really worries about being upstaged."

In addition, the director of the first two films, Tim Burton, has moved over to the producer's chair, leaving the helm to veteran Joel Schumacher, whose films include *The Incredible Shrinking Woman, St. Elmo's Fire, Lost Boys*, and *The Client*. Schumacher envisioned a brighter production design and a warmer, more vulnerable superhero in Kilmer. For the director, *Batman Forever* is an existential quest.

Schumacher described it as "a story about duality . . . Val struggling with whether or not Wayne and Batman can co-exist, Chris O'Donnell's Robin as a mirror of Bruce Wayne, and Kidman as a psychiatrist who specializes in dual personalities."

Batman Forever has a more varied palette," says screenwriter Akiva Goldsman, who worked with Schumacher in adapting John Grisham's *The Client* to the screen. Contrasting the dark, Gothic tone of the first two *Batman* movies, the screenwriter pointed out Schumacher's version has a "cascade of colors . . . The movie feels like a carnival ride. You get on at the top and you tumble down a hill very, very, very fast. And then—boom—you hit the ground. Hopefully, you'll come out of the theater going, 'Oh, my God! What just happened?' "

Schumacher returned to *Batman* creator Bob Kane's original 56-year-old comic book for his design ideas, as opposed to Burton, who preferred the gloomy ambience of the Dark Knight series, DC Comics' 1986 updating of the Caped Crusader story. "I went back to the comic books I fell in love with."

Goldsman insists the movie will defy expectations by giving a "heightened reality" to Gotham City. "We also wanted to give due time to the psychology of people whose response to having their parents killed is to become an avenger."

The modern touches include having Robin sport an earring and drive a Harley while the 40-pound batsuits (one of which comes with molded nipples) have sleeker, more sensual curves.

"You put this thing on and you want to inflict pain because it's so cumbersome," says Kilmer.

"The suit has been redesigned to more directly echo human musculature," says Goldsman, who adds the film is "very, very sexy." "You really believe that those are his muscles underneath. And you see the suit coming off, and you see the bruised and battered Bruce Wayne. That, obviously, involves you in a more human, and potentially, more erotic way. Joel makes any human being look the best he or she possibly can on screen, and that should have no small amount of panting in the seats."

With his punk butch-cut, leering grin, and skintight lime bodysuit adorned with question marks (said Schumacher: "Jim could not eat one scintilla of food," just as Carrey himself had predicted at Cannes the year before), Carrey fits the

Riddler like a glove. He is one of two villains, along with Tommy Lee Jones's Two-Face and his two molls, Sugar and Spice, played by Drew Barrymore and Debi Mazar.

Goldsman praises the film's nonstop action, calling it the cinematic equivalent of a kid in a sweet shop. "One way of doing that is by crafting characters . . . that make you want to keep coming back to them. Just when you think that you're going to get closure . . . with one character, you move on to the next. And that's very exciting. Our hope is that each scene will give you something new."

The movie, which opened June 16, 1995, gives Gotham City two new villains in Tommy Lee Jones's former D.A. Harvey Dent a.k.a. Two-Face and Jim Carrey's cybergenius Edward Nygma a.k.a. the Riddler, who join forces to brainwash the citizenry while Batman's alter ego Bruce Wayne undergoes some therapy with Nicole Kidman's drop-dead gorgeous criminal psychiatrist Chase Meridian. In his fight against crime to save the city, Batman takes on a new partner, Chris (*Scent of a Woman*) O'Donnell's young circus acrobat, also stricken by tragedy and reborn as his famed sidekick Robin.

Schumacher brought the film in on schedule

and under budget, which made the people at Warner Bros. extremely happy.

Screenwriter Goldsman couldn't believe how fast Schumacher shot the movie. "I really don't understand how his mind works. We had an obscene number of set-ups in any given day. I mean, the Batcave was actual size . . . can you imagine what lighting that thing was like?"

Batman Forever would be the fourth hit film in a row for Carrey, though his presence was hardly the difference in the successful series, but it obviously didn't hurt to have him aboard as a little added insurance. Unfortunately, his superstar status apparently caused friction on the set. The *L.A. Daily News* reported that the "dark, brooding" Val Kilmer was experiencing the same fears which reportedly drove Michael Keaton from the project—the specter of Jim Carrey's star power. Not only did Kilmer supposedly feel paranoid about Carrey "stealing the movie out from under him," he had a "hard time" handling Carrey's "bubbly ego."

But *Entertainment Weekly* made the situation sound like it wasn't all Jim's fault, that it was spawned by the fawning atmosphere that surrounds any superstar. Said co-star Chris O'Donnell: "Everyone would just stare and wait for him to say something funny. The minutes would tick by, and people were hovering and watching him. One day, Jim said, 'Hey, can I have a Diet Coke?' and ten people started roaring. It's like 'Ahhh! Jim Carrey asked for a Diet Coke. He just cracks us up!' Then he'd just sigh and go off to get his Coke himself."

By the spring of 1995, Jim Carrey had become more than a superstar actor; he had become a cottage industry. In February, he achieved the ultimate larger-than-life icon status when it was announced that all three of his films would be made into Saturday morning cartoon shows. ABC announced an animated version of *Dumb and Dumber* to debut in fall '95, while CBS announced cartoon productions of *The Mask* for September and *Ace Ventura: Pet Detective* for January '96. *Dumb and Dumber* and *The Mask* represented New Line TV's first two children's series based on hit movies and were being produced in association with sister Turner Broadcasting unit, Hanna-Barbera Cartoons and Sunbow Productions and Film Roman, respectively.

"He's struck a nerve as a new Jerry Lewis," says Mike Lazzo, head of programming and production at the cable Cartoon Network. "He's a big, exaggerated, dim-witted, slapstick personality. It's a natural to move that into cartoons."

CBS Vice President of Children's Programming and Daytime Specials, Judy Price agrees: "*Ace* is a perfect property to do detective stories with characters. It's a modern-day *Scooby Doo*."

The *Ace* cartoon does hold one trump card, with the rights to use Carrey's likeness for their series, unlike the animated version of *Dumb and Dumber*, which cannot portray either Carrey or co-star Jeff Daniels, or *The Mask*.

"Likeness is not an issue," New Line Television's Bob Friedman insists of the cartoon version of *Dumb and Dumber*. "The series will be about sensibility and style, and we hope it will communicate the level of dumbness that the feature was communicating."

CBS' Price says Carrey's likeness was not necessary for *The Mask*, either, since the title character is already a cartoon. As for how much he was making from all this, Carrey publicist Marleah Leslie claimed: "He's not involved in the cartoons. But I won't discuss his financial matters."

Carrey moved into the multimedia sphere in May, when New Line New Media published a CD-ROM entitled *Behind the Mask*, a look at the making of the hit movie. The interactive disc allows you to read the screenplay, browse through production stills, and see and hear interviews with the cast and crew.

The CD-ROM also takes you through the creative process. For the scene in which Carrey turns into a wolf, the viewer will see the Tex Avery original which inspired the segment, read the script excerpt, see the storyboards, watch how the special effects were accomplished, and then take a look at the final, completed version.

"It's like running away to join the circus," said *Mask* director Charles Russell. "There is a sense that we have the opportunity to do something more colorful and different than what films usually offer."

In March, Carrey took some time out with girlfriend Lauren Holly and good friend Nicolas Cage to celebrate songwriter pal Phil Roy's birthday at the House of Blues in Los Angeles, where they caught a show by Tuck & Patti, who performed their song "Heaven Down Here." It was a great night for Jim, who felt comfortable surrounded by good friends.

"We had known each other 10–12 years," said Roy. "And you know what? It coulda been eight years ago. Has the success changed him? He's a lot richer. A lot healthier. He's in amazing shape. The things that have changed are pretty obvious. He's one of the most successful people in the world right now. Basically, he worked for it. What I know better than anyone is that he worked really hard. And he knows what it was like not to have. Know what I mean? It didn't happen overnight. He's 33 now. The thing about it is, the people have just recently caught on to him. But he's always been this funny!"

As Carrey himself told more than one reporter about his "overnight success" after 15 years: "If it had happened when I was 21, I probably would have blown my brains out. Unless I had gone through all that disappointment, I don't think I would feel like I deserve it. As it is, I still every once in a while think, 'Oooh, what if they take it away?' "

And while he didn't forget his old friends nor where he came from, the overzealous attention of strangers every now and then bugged him, as did the harsh treatment his divorce was receiving in the tabloids.

When he went to Tokyo in March to promote the release of *The Mask*, he conducted a sobering press conference which revealed a different side to Jim Carrey.

"People come up to me expecting me to be funny and they're always surprised if I hit them with something heavy," he told the Japanese press. "I'm basically just a good faker."

In talking about the theme of *The Mask*, he alluded to his well-publicized marital split: "We need to put on a mask when we walk out the door in the morning. And be whatever we think people want us to be."

New Line could have signed Jim Carrey up for the sequel to *Ace Ventura* for a million bucks, but they balked, so the price had ballooned up to between $5 and $7 million when they finally anted up. By the time Carrey appeared on Barbara Walters' show on the night of the Oscars, he had just inked an agreement to star in *The Mask II* for a cool $10 million, which fulfilled his own prediction on that check he signed what seemed like ages ago.

Originally slated to be called *Ace Ventura, Pet Detective: Curse of the Wahiti*, then simply *Ace Ventura Goes to Africa*, the sequel probably switched locations to San Antonio, Texas and Charleston, South Carolina when Carrey's asking price went north. The name was then changed to *Ace Ventura: When Nature Calls*, which seemed to continue Carrey's obsession with bodily functions and animals, while supermodel Naomi Campbell was cast as his love interest.

Tapped to direct the movie was 34-year-old unproduced screenwriter Tom DeCerchio, a former ad copywriter and TV commercial director who got the nod to helm the movie on the basis of a 20-minute film called *Nunzio's Second Cousin*, a dark comedy about a gay Italian cop named John Randazzo (Vincent D'Onofrio) who brings a violent, gay-bashing teenager (Miles Perlich) home for dinner with his nutty, clueless mother (Eileen Brennan).

"People either love it or hate it," says De-Cerchio about the movie which got him his big break. "Which I'm told is a good thing. Nobody says, 'That's nice.' They either say, 'Wow! Let's have a meeting,' or they totally avoid taking my phone calls."

In 1991, DeCerchio was a co-founder of his own hot "brat pack" ad agency when he decided to pack it in and move to L.A. to write screenplays. He began directing TV commercials while out west, including the famed series of "Yes I Am" Bud Light spots with the men dressed as women in the pool hall, the guy who pilfers a limo ride, and the family reunion.

With the help of his ICM agents, DeCerchio's feature script for *Nunzio* attracted D'Onofrio and Brennan and an executive producer who "pulled in a lot of favors" to put together a crew of 50 for the three-day shoot.

"The things I learned in advertising are totally

applicable to the movie business," he said. "Because marketing is a major part of it. If you understand that, you're ahead of the pack."

On the basis of the success of *Nunzio* at the Sundance Film Festival in Park City, Utah, DeCerchio was hired by Warner Bros./Morgan Creek to direct the *Ace Ventura* sequel. He is now looking for backing to make his second feature, *Weaponsville*, a *Dr. Strangelove*-type comedy about gun control. The screenwriter for *Ace Ventura II*, in one more example of Jim Carrey's loyalty to old colleagues, is his *In Living Color* buddy, Steve Oedekerk, who was creative consultant on the first *Ace* movie and the guy who convinced Jim to appear in his one-man 1991 effort, *High Strung*.

Rushing back-to-back from one movie to another—he was planning on jumping right into *The Mask II* after completing the second *Ace* movie—Carrey had little time to pursue some of the artistic activities he developed in those years he stepped away from show business.

He took up painting and produced a pair of oil canvasses called "Imagining Ghosts" and "To Envy the Perfect Soul." He hung the latter behind a conference table in his business manager's office. It's a rendering of two angels, one ethereally blue, the other flesh-colored with big floppy feet and shrunken wings, struggling to climb to heaven, a perfect expression of the Carrey dichotomy.

He told a *Newsweek* reporter it symbolized the fact, if he didn't need anything from this earth, he could move on, adding immediately, "But I need a lot."

When Barbara Walters visited his house to interview him, Carrey showed her his sculptures, including one called "The Insomniac," a single bloodshot eyeball sitting on a pair of legs, representing Carrey's restless nature and own sleepless nights. Reminiscent of the "Rat Fink" character created by hot-rod artist "Big Daddy" Ed Roth, it is the kind of creation that caused Carrey's sister to ask him if he were all right when she visited him and saw several of the strange figures he had sculpted in the period of the mid-'80s when he walked away from show business.

And then there's, of course, Carrey's musical career—his songwriting partnership with Phil Roy and his singing/performing—an element he showed off to such great praise in *The Mask*.

Jim Carrey is a man of many faces and facets of his personality, like the mercurial changes he undergoes in *The Mask*. The wacky life of the party and class clown has a dark side that lurks just below the surface.

He pointed out that there was an edge, a danger, an anxiety and an anger to his work. "Even the guys I play in the movies, the nice guys, put their foot down. People are attracted to that. They identify with it."

Once again, he turns to one of his all-time favorite movies, *Mr. Smith Goes to Washington*, to make a point.

"I want to be Mr. Smith. I don't think I'll ever get there. He's a hero, not an ego. Mr. Smith is so honest he can't let anything go by. As a comedian you sit in judgment of everything that goes on in the world."

Still, he insists his comedy is more about escapism than dwelling on life's inequities, trying to forget the pain of life by reducing it to laughter.

Jim Carrey seeks that escapism in his work. From the time he was a brash 22-year-old who had just received his first starring TV role in *The Duck Factory*, Jim has been obsessed with work.

"Comedy started out as my hobby, and then it became my profession," he told *Interview* back in 1984, comparing it to "being on call all the time . . . with a built-in beeper . . . It's different from most other businesses in that way. You can't just leave the office and relax because you never know when you'll think of something funny."

Eleven years later, as one of Hollywood's top stars, Carrey is still driven by that hunger, the memory of the hard times, the obstacles—personal and professional—he had to overcome to get to where he is today. He told *Newsweek* he wasn't ready to sit back and "fill the garden," but he might be "ten years from now."

Of course, even all that success couldn't gnaw away at those insecurities.

He revealed he still had nightmares about ending up in a sitcom called *Jim's Place*, where he was "an intergalactic cop who crashed into the Chicago River and meets up with an earthling cop and solves crimes." He cautioned an interviewer, if he ever heard he had signed up to do *Ace Ventura 5*, to call him up and "remind [him] to put a bullet in his head."

ELEVEN

Can He Carrey On?: The Comic Superstar's Future and a Critical Assessment

"High in the Himalayas lives the Guru of Low Comedy, surrounded by his tapes of Laurel and Hardy, W.C. Fields and the brothers Zucker. 'Great Master, what is the secret of a hit?' ask Hollywood's best and richest when they are ushered into his presence. 'Make 'em laugh,' is the inevitable reply, 'any damn way you can.'"
—Richard Schickel, *Time*, review of *Dumb and Dumber*

Top Ten Things That Will Happen to Jim Carrey in The Next Decade

1. He'll be signed as a recording star and make a totally serious album . . . which will bomb like Eddie Murphy's.
2. He will do a remake of *It's a Wonderful Life* in the Jimmy Stewart role and critics will long for the "earlier, funnier Jim Carrey."
3. He will make a feature-length movie about Fire Marshall Bill called *I'm on Fire*.
4. He will eventually become the writer and director of his own movies, which will lead to a French commendation from the Minister of Culture.

5. His paintings and sculptures will be the subject of a one-person show at a prestigious Santa Monica gallery, where they will sell for outlandish sums.

6. His daughter will grow up to write a "Daddy Dearest" book about him.

7. He and Damon Wayans will do a buddy-buddy cop movie together.

8. *Hard Copy* will reveal his schlong rivals Milton Berle in size and no one will deny it.

9. DreamWorks will try to sign him to a contract which dwarfs all previous deals given to stars, offering to add a "C" to the SKG logo.

10. He'll sign to do *Ace Ventura 5* and shoot himself in the head (as he predicted he'd do in *Entertainment Weekly* back in 1995, before the magazine replaced *The New York Times* as the "paper of record" in 2010.)

So who is Jim Carrey, really? And what does his popularity tell us about America and the rest of the world in 1995, poised on the precipice of a multimedia future composed of technological haves and have-nots? Is he the death of literate civilization as we know it? Or merely the latest in a long line of court jesters who made us laugh to forget the pain? Is he a worthy successor to the physical comic genius of Chaplin, Keaton, Lloyd, Tati, and Sellers or merely Jerry Lewis Lite? So far, the critics have not been kind . . . but it's early yet and those elite who rely on the printed word to make a living have never shown an appreciation of the mass appeal form of slapstick and physical comedy. Still, even when Jim Carrey's movies have been savaged as "puerile" and devoid of verbal wit, the star has been grudgingly admired . . . even by his critics.

"The critical drubbing is from people who want generic Ellen DeGeneres rip-off crap," said his long-time pal and comic colleague Joey Gaynard. "Jim's true appeal comes from the box office. They can say whatever they want about slapstick. It never hurt Red Skelton. Or Gene Wilder. Or the early cast of *Saturday Night Live*. I love slapstick and Jimmy's just great at it. . . ."

But is he worth the cool $10 million per picture he's commanding, a figure that's undoubtedly headed higher in the near future? That's a lot easier to answer. In this multimedia era of video-on-demand, Jim Carrey is more than a triple-threat: aside from his commercial appeal—he may be the only actor capable of opening a film on his name alone, above even Tom Hanks and Arnold Schwarzenegger—he is the perfect '90s video star in the age of mechanical reproduction.

Unlike verbal comedies or spoken word bits, Carrey's physical antics don't diminish, they grow over multiple viewings . . . especially with the added home technology of stop-action and frame-by-frame offered by VCR and soon-to-be common technologies like laser disc. The pure joy of slapstick is in the repetition . . . and what better way to repeat than with that rewind button. This is an unprecedented opportunity at the crossroads of art and technology—and Jim Carrey's fool is right in the middle of it. Toss in the fact that each of Carrey's first four films have spawned a veritable self-generated economy of CD-ROMs, video games, books, tapes, and the old standard lunchboxes, and you can see how far we've come since the days of the Davy Crockett caps. Jim Carrey is the ultimate Boomer movie star in that he's a one-man merchandising machine that can't help but reach the Gen X'ers and post-X'ers alike . . . a man talking out of his asshole has a universality that even the Rolling Stones lack these days.

Jim Carrey's physical humor comes at a time when the world is tired of the unending stream of words and information being pumped through our tired systems. Carrey is the fly in the ointment, the absurdity that puts a stop to deadening logic, a guy who loves animals, still believes in romance, and isn't afraid to make a complete fool of himself in the pursuit of it. That's a character who can be very appealing in a time when duplicitousness and racial hatred are the order of the day, even in our laughs. Jim Carrey's beauty is the way he allows us to feel superior to him, the color-blind and childlike simplicity he brings to the table. The divine fool has long been a potent symbol for our civilization. It just seems we need him now more than ever.

"Of course, it's not very nice to laugh at mental deficiency," wrote Harold Schechter, a professor of American literature and culture at New York's Queens College in an *L.A. Times* op-ed piece defending Carrey's brand of juvenile high jinx. "But 'Idiot Jokes' are actually part of a widespread and ancient folklore tradition.

"Throughout the world, in all times and places, a significant number of folk tales have dealt with the comical doings of dimwits, buffoons and imbeciles. Folklorists call these anecdotes numskull stories."

As Schechter goes on to explain, the success of Carrey's movies is not an example of a "dumbing down of America," but simply the contemporary expression "of a figure that has delighted people throughout the ages. Ultimately, their popularity tells us less about the present state of American culture than about the unchanging needs of the human imagination."

Or, as Richard Shickel put it in his *Time* review of *Dumb and Dumber*: "In order to enjoy the pair's company, adult viewers must regress to those thrilling days of yesteryear when bodily dysfunction represented the height of hilarity. [But] Carrey is both symbol and satirist of our apparently irresistible dumbing down. Astonished attention must be paid."

That's right. The idiot—like the title character of Fyodor Dostoyevsky's classic work—with his disregard for society's conventions and decorum, permits the audience its own vicarious release of our own libidinous fantasies and hidden id-like urges. Just as Carrey's Lloyd Christmas dreams of assassinating his beloved's husband, yet holds back on that murderous impulse to be "normal" and "civilized."

That dualism between mind and body, thought and action, impulse and response, weakness and strength, knowledge and stupidity, ice and fire, heaven and hell—is at the core of Carrey's lapsed Catholic viewpoint.

"The comedy doesn't only push off from a dark past," he told the *Boston Globe*. "I guess there is a lot of that, but there's also a carefree aspect. It's like my escape, you know? A way not to take things so seriously. So it's free-associating and riffs and stuff, but also just complete bull. Y'know, I'll start a story about how I was attacked by a great white shark and, of course, the audience knows it's not true, but they don't care. It's like sometimes you'll be fighting with your girlfriend, or something, and you realize in the middle of it, you say to yourself, 'Right now, I could turn it off and start laughing.' But that wouldn't work, either, because it'd probably bug her even more. But sometimes, you're way out here, lookin' at it happen, and it really doesn't have to happen."

Or, as he put it more simply, "I live in my head . . . I seriously do."

And now millions of other people have lived inside Jim Carrey's head and found it's a place where they can forget their own problems.

"The coarse, even obscene antics of the fool have been celebrated in countless performances throughout the world, from the Feast of Fools of medieval Europe to the rituals of Native American clown societies," wrote Professor Schechter. "It may be painful to acknowledge but—like another pair of modern-day numskulls, Beavis and Butt-head—the moronic heroes of *Dumb and Dumber* spring from psychic sources common to us all . . . Oh, yes. And one more thing. They are really, really funny."

What the good professor reminds us is, cut through all the psychological mumbo-jumbo and what Jim Carrey is is FUNNY. He makes us laugh. Like the proverbial class clown, which he was, he punctures the proceedings with something that cracks us up. And funny is, basically, indescribable. It simply is. Break it down into its component parts, and it ceases to be the thing that hits our funnybone.

Jim Carrey's Ten Funniest Bits

1. Fire Marshall Bill
2. His "Oscar acceptance speech" in *The Mask*
3. Kicking the box as the delivery boy in *Ace Ventura*
4. His karate dream sequence in *Dumb and Dumber*
5. Talking out of his asshole in *Ace Ventura*
6. Walking into a pick-up bar at a right angle in *Jim Carrey's Unnatural Act*
7. His James Dean impression in *Earth Girls Are Easy*
8. Cleansing himself after the "Crying Game" experience in *Ace Ventura*

9. Getting ready to go out on the town in *The Mask*
10. Running slow motion in a tutu in *Ace Ventura*

Jim Carrey climbed to the top of the comedy heap in 1994, setting box office records when his three films topped the $300-million mark. A comedian hasn't had a string like that since Eddie Murphy lit up with *Trading Places, 48 Hours* and *Beverly Hills Cop*, but the former *Saturday Night Live* star couldn't sustain that pace. You'd have to go back to Richard Pryor or Cheech & Chong, perhaps, to find another comic who has hit such a commercially successful formula. Can Carrey keep it up? Or will he turn out to be like Jerry Lewis, gradually losing touch with his audience until no one cares?

Even Lewis himself has advice for Jim, whom he describes as "the best visual comic to come down the pike in years," but criticizes *Dumb and Dumber* for its scatological humor: "All those toilet jokes? If Carrey would like a shortcut to career suicide, get dirty, get sleazy. His longevity will be cut by 20 years."

Of course, Jerry wasn't too proud to hint at a possible on-screen match-up with his dufus dopelgänger. "It's a father-son deal," he told an *En-*

tertainment Weekly reporter. "Naturally, I'm going to play the son." Budda-bing, budda-boom. Cymbal crash and out.

Right now, just as a pure improvisatory mimic, Jim Carrey rivals Robin Williams, but his physical dexterity and grace puts the more lumbering Williams to shame.

"Carrey's many things, but he's neither simple nor mediocre," wrote *Newsday* critic Gene Seymour, the same man who had so much trouble defining the man's appeal in his review of *Dumb and Dumber* quoted earlier in the book. "Anyone who watched his work on *In Living Color* could have told you this well before the release of *Ace* last year. [But] silliness-for-its-own sake has never been easily understood by sober-minded reviewers who prefer to have a theme or a moral attached to their stories. The public is another matter. They'll take funny stuff wherever they can get it."

At the moment, Jim Carrey is the Great Slapstick Hope. He has risen to the top of the pile not overnight, but through 16 years of hard work and determination.

As he told Barbara Walters when she asked if he ever got discouraged when he was booed during that first appearance at Yuk-Yuk's in the yellow polyester suit his mother made him wear:

"You kind of develop a thick skin when it comes to being ridiculed. I couldn't give it up . . . I didn't have any other trait or skill."

Or as Steve Allen told the *L.A. Times*: "Forty years ago, there were maybe 50 comedians at a given time who could do whatever it was they did. There was more space to be original. Now, the number's more like 5,000 and it's awfully hard for a younger person to define himself or herself as being truly original enough to break away from the pack."

Jim Carrey was one who did. He fought his way through the thickets of just that over-populated comedy club circuit to make his mark, refusing merely to be good at being an impressionist, he had the cajones to chuck it all and start all over with something uniquely his. The dreams he had of being special were finally realized. Jim Carrey went from being trapped inside his head to plying his trade for millions around the world. And what is the key to his success? Can anybody explain the mystery of Carrey's appeal?

"Mystery," says Allen. "That's the precise word. It's easy to describe somebody as funny. It's the why that's difficult and, perhaps, impossible."

TWELVE

What Makes Carrey Run?
Ten Reasons Why

WHEN I first started this book, my opinion of Jim Carrey was probably much like a lot of yours. That the guy was a prime example of all that was wrong with today's mass-market popular culture and Hollywood lowest-common-denominator vulgarity. That he was just another *Wayne's World*-meets-"Beavis & Butt-head" yahoo playing to the "Ernest" crowd with one or two caricatures and a Lorne Michaels production deal. That he was the white guy on *In Living Color* and well, what else has he done? I mean, the Marx Brothers and the Three Stooges were seminal influences in my own childhood, but I eventually grew to appreciate the sophisticated wit and urbane dialogue of a Preston Sturges,

Roy Trakin

Frank Capra, Woody Allen, or Billy Wilder. Of course, Carrey could negate all of 'em by uttering out of his butt-cheeks: "You're talking like an a-hole, wienie."

Given a chance to observe the 16-year climb it took Jim Carrey to get to where he is today gave me a great deal more respect for the guy. Seeing how he parlayed small roles, which he tried to make his own into increased visibility, all the while honing his craft, until the moment he was ready to explode was impressive. His subtle, underrated filmwork created memorable, if small characterizations in *Peggy Sue Got Married*, *The Dead Pool*, and *Earth Girls Are Easy*. He proved he could do feckless, virginal, straight man leads in the tradition of his idol Dick Van Dyke in the likes of the otherwise forgettable *Once Bitten* as well as a pitifully underutilized stint on *The Duck Factory*. He showed he could play drama with the critically praised role in the Fox TV-movie, *Doing Time on Maple Drive*. His improvisatory work in *Jim Carrey's Unnatural Act* and throughout his work on *In Living Color* fully prepared him for the spontaneity which has made his three movies such fresh hits.

More importantly, Jim Carrey has become a superstar without forgetting the people along the way, too. One thing which impressed me was the level of loyalty he inspired in his friends. People like Yuk-Yuk's owner Mark Breslin and Morgan Creek Chairman James Robinson wouldn't talk unless permission was granted by Jim's very zealous publicist, Marleah Leslie. Old pals like Joey Gaynard and Phil Roy go out of their way to stress what a regular, down-to-earth guy Carrey has remained despite his success. Of course, you probably wouldn't hear such tales from Jim's first wife, Melissa, who has steadfastly refused to go public with her side of the dispute which promises to rage on tabloid TVs when the divorce proceedings go public sometime later this year. Carrey's making lots of money and inquiring minds claim he doesn't want his ex-wife to get her hands on more of it than he feels she's entitled to.

There are some who feel Jim Carrey could be his generation's Jimmy Stewart. Of course, given the high stakes present in today's entertainment business, he could be a lot more. If he gets the right script. And the right role. The sky's the limit for Jim Carrey. And he deserves it, too. After all, he worked for it.

Top Ten Reasons for Jim Carrey's Success

1. **He's from Canada:** Everyone knows people
   from Canada are just naturally funny. John
   Candy, Dan Aykroyd, Mike Myers, Paul
   Shaffer, Tommy Chong, Howie Mandel, Rich
   Little, Phil Hartman, Mack Sennett, Mort
   Sahl, Martin Short, David Steinberg, and the
   Kids in the Hall all came from the North
   Country. It gives you that outsider's perspective. It probably made Carrey try that
   much harder when he was an unknown toil-
   ing at the Comedy Store. He surely used his
   Canadian underdog status as the topic of the
   opening bit in *Jim Carrey's Unnatural Act*,
   quickly getting the Toronto audience on his
   side.

2. **His father, Percy:** Carrey never failed to admit that it was his dad's humor and his own
   trying to make his dad laugh which were the
   two most important factors that shaped his
   early childhood. Inadvertently, it was his
   dad's failure to live up to his own dreams as
   an entertainer which fueled his son's ambition to succeed. If there was a culminating
   moment in the first 33 years of Jim Carrey's
   life, it would be the moment he placed in his

father's casket that ersatz $10 million check he made out to himself.

3. **That first night at Yuk-Yuk's when he bombed:** From the fluorescent yellow tuxedo his mother forced him to wear, and his father driving him to the club while working on his act with him, to Yuk-Yuk's owner Mark Breslin playing the "Jesus Christ Superstar" tape as the crowd screamed, "Crucify him! Crucify him!," Jim Carrey's comic debut was certainly a religious experience, a horribly humiliating epiphany which led to him staying away from clubs for the next two years ... during which time he crafted an act with his dad and proceeded to become the toast of Toronto.

4. **Moving to L.A. and getting discovered by Rodney Dangerfield:** It took a great deal of courage for young Jim Carrey to pick himself up out of the seminomadic existence he had in Toronto, to move away from his poverty-stricken family, and try his hand at Hollywood. Rodney Dangerfield should be recognized as the patron saint of young comics for what he did for Jim, exposing him to the circuit and giving Jim exposure as his opening act. It was something Carrey would always be grateful for. The Comedy Store be-

Roy Trakin

came his home away from home, where he met the group of people he remains friends with to this day, including his wife, Melissa.

5. **Landing *The Duck Factory*:** Getting a national TV sitcom so early in your career and then flopping might have been a career setback for some, but it merely confirmed what Jim Carrey knew along—he should be in control of his own destiny and not subject to the whims of others. He also learned that commercial television was a dead end if he really wanted to be creative. He would refuse to do any until hooking up with *In Living Color* seven years later.

6. **Giving up stand-up comedy for two years to re-tool his act:** If Jim Carrey hadn't decided to give up his budding stand-up career at its height, he might be a "musical impressionist" opening for Whitney Houston at the MGM Grand in Las Vegas. Everyone told him he was crazy ditching what had been a successful act simply to disappear, but the two years Carrey spent exploring his inner self, branching out into painting and sculpture, deciding to let loose and "spew," helped him create the major elements of the Jim Carrey persona we know today.

7. **Getting a role in *Earth Girls Are Easy* and**

becoming friends with Damon Wayans: No one saw the movie, of course, but it just goes to show what professionalism, and trying to create something out of nothing, gets you, as Carrey puts his heart and soul into the character of the fuzzy Wiploc alien, which impresses co-alien Damon Wayans, who tells brother Keenen Ivory Wayans about the angry cat with the improvisatory bent who would be perfect for him to . . .

8. **Cast in *In Living Color*:** For all intents and purposes, the big break in Jim Carrey's career, the chance for him to emblazon his series of brilliant characterizations on the mind of the American public. Carrey thrived in the creative atmosphere, once again the cultural outsider, but someone whose outrage crossed racial lines, just as it did the lines of reason and sanity. The following he built up in the Fox show enabled him to snare the lead role in a comedy that had seemingly passed through every actor's hands in Hollywood. His Fire Marshall Bill's a classic.

9. **The opening weekend's box office gross for *Ace Ventura*:** In this age of the information superhighway, news travels fast and stars are made overnight. That was the story the weekend of February 4, 1995, when the little-

heralded *Ace Ventura: Pet Detective* grossed an astounding $12 million, thereby changing the life of Jim Carrey forever. A star was born.

10. **Getting the part of the Riddler in *Batman Forever*:** Up until now, Jim Carrey has been the province of the cultists. Of course, those same cultists now number in the millions and have contributed $300-million plus to his film's box office grosses. With *Batman Forever*, even those who turned up their noses at *Ace Ventura* and *Dumb and Dumber* will come around. Jim Carrey's Riddler has the feel of the kind of scene-stealer that Jack Nicholson's Joker was in the first *Batman*, and if that's the case, Jim Carrey's streak goes to four in a row with no end in sight.

Jim Carrey Filmography

1983: *Club Med*
Starring: Alan Thicke, Bill Maher, Rita Coolidge
Directed by: David Mitchell

1984: *Finders Keepers*
Starring: Michael O'Keefe, Beverly D'Angelo,
  Louis Gossett, Jr.
Directed by: Richard Lester

1985: *Once Bitten*
Starring: Lauren Hutton, Cleavon Little
Directed by: Howard Storm
Studio/Video: Samuel Goldwyn/Vestron Video
Plays: Mark Kendall, virginal ice cream man

1986: *Peggy Sue Got Married*
Starring: Kathleen Turner, Nicolas Cage
Directed by: Francis Ford Coppola
Studio/Video: Tri-Star/CBS Fox
Plays: Walter Getz, doo-wop dentist

1988: *The Dead Pool*
Starring: Clint Eastwood, Liam Neeson
Directed by: Buddy Van Horn
Studio/Video: Warner Bros./Warner Home
    Video
Plays: Johnny Shakes, wasted rock star

1989: *Pink Cadillac*
Starring: Clint Eastwood, Bernadette Peters
Directed by: Buddy Van Horn
Studio/Video: Warner Bros./Warner Home
    Video
Plays: Unnamed nightclub comic doing Elvis
    impression

1989: *Earth Girls Are Easy*
Starring: Geena Davis, Jeff Goldblum, Julie
    Brown
Directed by: Julien Temple
Studio/Video: Vestron Pictures/Vestron Home
    Video
Plays: Wiploc (Alien #2)

1992: *Doing Time on Maple Drive*
Starring: James B. Sikking, Bibi Besch, Lori
    Loughlin
Directed by: Ken Olin
Studio: FNM Movies (made for Fox-TV)
Plays: Tim Carter, alcoholic son

1994: *Ace Ventura: Pet Detective*
Co-Starring: Sean Young, Courtney Cox
Directed by: Tom Shadyac
Studio/Video: Warner Bros./Warner Home
    Video
Plays: Ace Ventura, Pet Detective
Salary: $350,000

1994: *The Mask*
Co-Starring: Cameron Diaz, Richard Jeni, Peter
    Riegert
Directed by: Charles Russell
Studio/Video: New Line/New Line Home
    Video
Plays: Stanley Ipkiss, timid bank teller turned
    manic superhero
Salary: $450,000

1994: *Dumb and Dumber*
Co-Starring: Jeff Daniels, Lauren Holly
Directed by: Peter Farrelly

Studio/Video: New Line/New Line Home
   Video
Plays: Lloyd Christmas, dimwit
Salary: $7 million

1995: *Batman Forever*
Starring: Val Kilmer, Nicole Kidman, Tommy
   Lee Jones
Directed by: Joel Schumacher
Studio/Video: Warner Bros./Warner Home
   Video
Plays: The Riddler, arch-enemy
Salary: $5 million

1995: *Ace Ventura II: When Nature Calls*
Co-Starring: Naomi Campbell
Directed by: Tom DeCerchio
Studio/Video: Warner Bros./Warner Home
   Video
Plays: Ace Ventura, Pet Detective
Salary: $5–$7 million

1995: *The Mask II*
Starring: Jim Carrey
Studio/Video: New Line/New Line Home
   Video
Plays: Stanley Ipkiss
Salary: $10 million

Also appeared on: NBC-TV series, *The Duck Factory* ('84), episode of *Buffalo Bill* (TV) *Comedy Store Special* (HBO), *In Living Color* (Fox TV), and *Jim Carrey's Unnatural Act* (Showtime)

ABOUT THE AUTHOR

ROY Trakin is a popular culture critic, pop music aficionado and diehard Mets/Knicks/Jets fan who is now exiled in the San Fernando Valley paying off the SBA loan on the earthquake-ravaged house he shares with his indispensable wife, Jill Merrill, and his two auteurist children, Taylor Max and Tara Paige, who know more about Jim Carrey than any seven- and five-year-old have a right to know. Trakin is the senior editor of *HITS*, has contributed to every rock magazine that ever mattered (*Musician, BAM*, the old *Creem* and old *Details, New York Rocker, Soho Weekly News*, etc.) and has previously written *Sting and the Police* (Ballantine Books, '84) and *Tom Hanks: Journey to Stardom* (St. Martin's Press, '95). He was also an editorial assistant on *John Lennon Remembered: Strawberry Fields Forever* (Bantam Books, '80).

Alcatraz. The prison fortress off the coast of San Francisco. No man had gotten out alive before his time was up, until a 20-year-old petty thief named Willie Moore broke out.

Recaptured, then thrown into a pitch-black hellhole for three agonizing years, Willie is driven to near-madness—and finally to a brutal killing. Now, up on first-degree murder charges, he must wrestle with his nightmares and forge an alliance with Henry Davidson, the embattled lawyer who will risk losing his career and the woman he loves in a desperate bid to save Willie from the gas chamber.

Together, Willie and Henry will dare the most impossible act of all: get Willie off on a savage crime that the system drove him to commit— and put Alcatraz itself on trial.

MURDER
IN THE FIRST

Dan Gordon

NOW A MAJOR MOTION PICTURE STARRING CHRISTIAN SLATER, KEVIN BACON, AND GARY OLDMAN

He's already blown up a subway. He's already sent the NYPD scrambling. Now, he's holding the entire city of New York hostage with the world's deadliest explosive— and he's making John McClane jump through hoops.

Once McClane was the best. Then he lost everything. Now, he's racing against the clock, following orders from a psycho bomber who's made massive destruction into a very personal game of revenge: when the city goes up, McClane will die first.

It can't happen. It won't happen. With a tough, streetwise partner, John McClane races across a panicked city, smashing the rules, locked and loaded for the ultimate duel...

DIE HARD
WITH A VENGEANCE

A novel by D. Chiel
Based on a screenplay written by Jonathan Hensleigh
Now a major motion picture
Starring Bruce Willis, Jeremy Irons and Samuel L. Jackson
and Directed by John McTiernan

_____ 95676-2 $4.99 U.S./$5.99 Can.

His inventive, off-the-wall humor made America laugh out loud in movies like *Big, Turner and Hooch*, and *A League of Their Own*. His charm and boyish good looks won over Darryl Hannah in *Splash* and Meg Ryan in *Sleepless in Seattle*. His genius for breathing life into a character made *Forrest Gump* a household name. And his haunting Oscar-winning performance in *Philadelphia* established him as one of today's hottest leading men.

Warm, witty and vulnerable, Tom Hanks is both the everyman we can all identify with and an actor with stunning star quality. Now, Roy Trakin traces Hanks' life and career in this honest, no-holds-barred biography.

TOM HANKS
JOURNEY TO STARDOM

ROY TRAKIN

TOM HANKS
Roy Trakin
_____ 95596-0 $4.99 U.S./$5.99 Can.